China's Great Classic

Over two thousand years ago, the wise, much-revered Chinese philosopher and teacher, Confucius, taught his simple truths about every aspect of life in pointed stories and clever aphorisms. *The Sayings of Confucius*, which comprise all of the four hundred and fifty recorded brief conversations and observations of the great sage, colorfully expound such basic virtues as a child's duty toward his parents, love between brothers, devotion to family tradition, reliability in friendships, loyalty to superiors, and justice to all men.

Living in an age of violent change, when China was dominated by feudal war lords, Confucius stressed the value of social cohesion and the importance of harmony. Full of wit and wisdom, *The Sayings of Confucius* are as pertinent today as 2000 years ago.

JAMES R. WARE, Associate Professor of Chinese at Harvard University and an authority on Chinese culture, has prepared this new and complete translation of *The Sayings of Confucius*. He has also provided an illuminating introduction which describes the times of Confucius, as well as a valuable chronological listing of Chinese dynasties from earliest history down to the present.

Other MENTOR Books of Special Interest

THE SAYINGS OF MENCIUS *translated by James R. Ware*
The wisdom of a great disciple of Confucius, as meaningful today as it was two thousand years ago. (#MD307—50¢)

THE SAYINGS OF CHUANG CHOU
translated by James R. Ware
A new translation of the writing of a successor of Confucius who led ancient China to a rebirth of progressive, dynamic Confucianism. (#MT543—75¢)

THE WAY OF LIFE: Tao Tê Ching *by Lao Tzu*
A new translation by R. B. Blackney of a masterpiece of ancient Chinese wisdom. (#MP416—60¢)

THE WHITE PONY: An Anthology of Chinese Poetry
edited by Robert Payne
A rich collection of Chinese poetry spanning over three thousand years and covering every conceivable mood and subject. (#MT301—75¢)

TO OUR READERS

The Sayings of
CONFUCIUS

A New Translation by
JAMES R. WARE

A Mentor Religious Classic
Published by THE NEW AMERICAN LIBRARY

MENTOR BOOKS are published *in the United States* by
The New American Library of World Literature, Inc.,
501 Madison Avenue, New York, New York 10022,
in Canada by The New American Library of Canada Limited,
156 Front Street West, Toronto 1, Ontario,
in the United Kingdom by The New English Library Limited,
Barnard's Inn, Holborn, London, E.C. 1, England

PRINTED IN THE UNITED STATES OF AMERICA

Contents

Introduction

Here is the historical Confucius (551-479 B.C.). Every quotation in this book not attributed directly or by context to another is to be assigned to him. Here is Confucius—as he has been learned by heart by every school child in China for well over two thousand years, from the time he became nationally orthodox, which at the latest was around 150 B.C. You can also discover Confucius as the ordinary, sincere, at times heartbroken, fallible teacher that he was. You can win from the perusal of this document some hint of the confidence he inspired in a handful of immediate followers. If the need is yours, you can also receive personal encouragement for the leading of the good life, because Confucius speaks to all men as man to man. Notice that Confucius has never been deified; he has only been revered by his countrymen as The First Teacher, The Sagest of the Sage. But he it was who inspired in all China the placid confidence in national custom and polite living which made her, much later, the civilizer of the whole Far East; he has been revered wherever Chinese culture has penetrated. Confucius has much to say to us today. Through him we could, if we so willed, achieve a more valid synthesis of the facts available to our generation—they are far more vast than ever before—and thus formulate for ourselves a better Truth.

China in the day of Confucius was a patriarchal society; it was a feudal society. The one and only concept of organization was paternalism and the large family; society did not sanction individual initiative. Persons at the very top were overseers only; those at the bottom could only be subjects. Between these two extremes, one was an overseer to all inferiors and a subject to all superiors. Man's highest respectable goal was service in the government. All that we know of education and the strivings of the time reveals the Chinese intent upon advancement within government service, for that group of intellectuals alone did the recording.

It is logical then that keen competition should have produced a corps of scholars offering preparation for governmental appointments. These teachers, revered as veritable parents, constituted a focal point for an oral tradition plus a certain amount of written legend or fact to be found in *The Poems* (*shih*) or *The Writings of Old* (*shu*), both of which have become part of the classical canon. These teachers stressed the cultivation of social and religious graces—both intimately intertwined—which were later formulated in a huge canon of detailed prescriptions known as *li,* which, lacking a better all-inclusive term, we normally translate as rites, etiquette, or good manners. With this code was also associated music. As a result nothing in social and religious intercourse was left to last-minute individual inspiration. For one born and bred to the system, life was as intricate—and as simple—as diplomatic protocol, where one does not innovate.

In the matter of religion Confucius' contemporaries recognized Sky, overseer of all things below, ghosts which were the spirits of the dead, and a multiplicity of divinities, demons, and fairies, personifications of objects and forces in nature. Confucius' own interests, however, were directed chiefly to the development in his pupils of a moral standard itself, not the techniques, as the best preparation for the good life and for public service. He seems to have played the double rôle of conservative and innovator; he invited his generation to maintain all the old official state religious practices—the popular religion he does not recommend to his social class—yet at the same time he advised them as to their dignity as human beings. The latter injunction was not clear to his listeners and he had constantly to define what he meant.

These social conditions had a political and legendary background centered in northern China's valley of the Yellow River and its tributaries. Confucius, a name resulting from the Latinization of K'ung fu-tzu—Master K'ung —flourished at a time when local civilization was dotted with city-states. These states varied widely in their geographical extents, though most, or all, had one or more metropolitan centers surrounded by a wall. Each state consisted also of countryside marked sporadically with small villages. There were no isolated farmhouses. A man belonged by birth to one of these states, but there was normally the possibility of permanent or temporary emigration to another, for there was a basic unity in culture and custom which enabled adjustment to local prejudice. Although numerous and widely scattered, despite constant bickering which frequently led to armed conflict, the states recognized that they formed a confederation whose cohesion was in direct proportion to the political and military power of a publicly recognized central authority (the King or Son of Sky). In the days of Confucius the Chinese people recognized that they were living under their third central authority. Six hundred years before, royal power had passed to a state called Chou. It was known that this dynasty had been preceded by one called Yin or Shang, and that there had been a first dynasty called Hsia. Legend related how the Hsia had been founded by Yü the Great, who had been preceded by two highly virtuous rulers named Yao and Shun. Confucius was conscious of and recognized himself as the intellectual successor to a cultural and institutional hero, the Duke of Chou, brother of the founder of the Chou dynasty.

By the year 500 B.C., however, the Chou dynasty, founded upon successful military action, was tottering. Its descendants had been succeeding one another for more than five centuries, and man's institutions often seem to reflect his own physical condition. Political and military decadence at the heart of the confederation was reflected in cultural life generally. All the princely families of consequence inevitably desired to succeed to the central royal power. In fact, the history of China from 500 to 250 B.C. is the story of the diplomatic and military efforts to determine this succession. It was the state of Ch'in in northwestern China which finally won. It not only succeeded to royal power, it founded the Chinese empire. So momentous was this event in eastern Asia that the name Ch'in long persisted in India and southeastern Asia, whence Western navigators brought it to Europe around 1500 to become the normal Western name for that part of the world, China. Meanwhile the Chinese had been designating their country by the name of their current dynasty, or by the epithet Chung-kuo—Middle Kingdom—which aptly expresses the Chinese nationalistic conception of geography.

The teacher Confucius seems to have been too ardent an idealist to have had a successful political career. When asked one day why he held no particular post in the political hierarchy, he was forced to the consoling explanation that even the man who leads, in private, a moral life can be considered an office-holder. On another occasion, wearied with the anarchy of his times, he yearned for appointment so that he might be enabled to create a new, strong, central authority—to be located near his own home in eastern China rather than in the west, where they had been founded in the past.

Was Confucius' success, then, due to the happy coincidence of time and an uncompromising insistence upon an ideal which reflected the basic common sense of the Chinese? A careful examination of history could show that many men have been as ardently devoted to an ideal as Confucius, Buddha, Socrates, Jesus, and Mohammed; yet their times presumably did not need them, for they became only followers in the train. Confucius himself claimed to be simply a follower of an ideal set by a paragon who flourished some five hundred years before his time. Yet by 100 B.C. he was called The First Teacher, The Sagest of the Sage, and succeeding centuries agreed. It is to his influence that China owes the founding of a tradition and the reverence which, after crystallization, became an orthodoxy for all literate Chinese.

Confucius was born into a China torn by political and cultural anarchy. It was an age when a subjective sophistry similar to that in the Greek tradition was impinging upon the objective traditions of the land. And it was Confucius who inspired a defense against these sophistic innovations by reasserting confidence in older principles and practices. Yet ancient China did perish in a welter of political contenders, each supported by preachers of new ideas and panaceas. In a later China, re-established out of materials preserved by her teachers, it was looked back upon as the age of the Philosophers. Among them there were at least three schools which could be associated with the teachings of the Master. The teachings of all three have survived in the form of collected writings: *Mo tzu, Meng tzu,* and *Hsün tzu.* Only the second—*Mencius*—was finally recognized as orthodox and became the thirteenth and last item in the Confucianist canon around A.D. 1100. The *Lun yü,* however, the book which is herewith translated into English under the title of *The Sayings of Confucius,* has been classical ever since China emerged from antiquity—one of the six classics carved upon stone between A.D. 175 and 183. The other five were *The Changes, The Writings of Old, The Poems, The Ceremonials,* and *The Annals* with the Kung-yang commentary.

The Chinese ideogram for the word "classic" belongs to the craft of weaving and would be translated literally by "warp"—that part of the fabric which is basic and fundamental, without which there would be neither weaving nor cloth. The books which the Chinese have recognized as constituting the very warp of their national cultural existence were, as we have seen, thirteen in number. There is repeated reference in the present text to *The Writings of Old* and *The Poems,* the second and third books in the canon. Number one in the list, *The Changes,* is mentioned, but one has the feeling that Confucius does not insist upon it. It appears to have belonged to the College of Diviners, to those in the community who were specialists in the domain of religion, and the form in which it has survived shows it to be a book of divination. Its core is sixty-four hexagrams, each composed of six straight lines, either whole or with one middle break, laid horizontally one above the other. They could very well be derived from one whole line, a symbol of *yang,* and one line broken at the middle, a symbol of *yin.* The varying combinations of these lines, first as digrams, then trigrams, and finally hexagrams, is at each step a maximum, and thus capable of being a symbolic representation of the whole universe. Its evolution ceased at the hexagram stage, and to each of these sixty-four there is attached a brief text, the whole mass of which was thought to bear upon matters of practical living. In order to divine the future a couple of these hexagrams with their accompanying texts are chosen by lot, and an expert has no difficulty in establishing a relation between the specific problem and the text, thanks to the special nature of the Chinese language. Thus he makes his recommendations. It goes without saying that the translation of such a text can never be definitive; the deciding factor must always be the question which is brought to it. *The Changes* also include a series of ten appendices, which deal with this system of divination and the classification of natural phenomena, and make an attempt to find a general system in nature. Three of these have been attributed to Confucius. In sum, it is a classic which offers nothing to us today, yet in China it is undoubtedly still being used for divination.

The Poems, which are so often referred to by Confucius, seem to have reached us in approximately the same form that he knew them. They are extremely valuable to the sociologist and anthropologist for their concrete references to the everyday life of those times and as the repositories of old legends. *The Sayings of Confucius* (*Lun yü*) are extraordinary in that they show the Chinese interpreting this collection of early poems as exhortations to high moral living. The late Professor Marcel Granet of Paris has given us a sympathetic study of the sociological and anthropological content of the poems, and Mr. Arthur Waley has published a translation (as *The Book of Songs*) which emphasizes its literary qualities. Later legend has made Confucius the editor of *The Poems*.

The Writings of Old, the second book in the canon, suffered most during the destructive period preceding the founding of the Chinese empire. As we now have it, it consists of a collection of laudatory diplomas and fragments of dramas based on exploits of the ancestors. It often goes under the misrepresentative English title of *The Book of History*. Legend has made Confucius the editor of this collection, as well.

Items four to six include writings on rites, protocol, and bureaucratic organization of government—the Chinese word is *li*. They are known as *Notes on the Rites* (*Li chi* or *Li ki*), *Cermonials* (*I li*), and *Chou li*, which is considered to be the ideal bureaucratic organization for the Chou dynasty (1100-250 B.C.). Confucius is not held to be the compiler of these collections, but he may well have known materials of this type. Although they are of little interest to any but scholars in the West today, in China they have been followed as guides to public and private ceremonies.

The seventh classic is *The Annals*, the Chinese *Ch'un-ch'iu*. The usual English title, *The Spring and Autumn Annals*, is one of those flowery renderings which is really meaningless, for while *ch'un* is spring and *ch'iu* is autumn, the combination in Chinese connotes the year. *The Annals* is a diary of the political events, including natural phenomena, between 722 and 481 B.C. as viewed from the state of Lu (southwest modern Shantung), the native state of Confucius. Tradition assigns the compilation of this book to Confucius, who is said to have had access to the state archives. It might be compared with the outline of history found in a large English dictionary. The Chinese hold this classic to be fundamental for all those who would rise high in the hierarchy and become expert in the art of government, and Chinese historians have used it as a model. *The Annals* has been preserved with three old commentaries: the *Tso chuan*, the *Kung-yang chuan* and the *Ku-liang chuan*.

Tenth in the list is the *Lun yü*—*The Sayings of Confucius*—which is translated here.

Number eleven, the *Hsiao ching*, is a very short conversation on filial duty. It is similar in form to the *Lun yü*, and its composition has been attributed to Confucius, but it looks more like a didactic piece by a less inspired teacher.

Number twelve goes by the untranslatable title of *Erh ya*. It is a topical collection of glosses on the many terms in the classics which must have proved difficult in Chinese antiquity, and it is the "ancestor" of a type of Chinese compilation by categories which corresponds somewhat with the encyclopedias of the West.

Mencius, number thirteen, is twice as long as the *Lun yü*. It is concerned chiefly with the travels and verbose teachings of the Confucianist Mencius (372-289 B.C.), and it gives evidence of the conflicts among the various schools of Confucius' followers.

When a Chinese speaks of the Classics, he uses such terms as the Five Classics and the Four Books. The former consists of *The Changes, The Writings of Old, The Poems, The Ceremonials* (or the *Li chi*, or both), and *The Annals* (generally accompanied by *Tso chuan*). The latter term has been used only from about A.D. 1200 and is largely associated with the name of the teacher and statesman Chu Hsi (1130-1200). The Four Books are *Lun yü, Mencius,* and two short chapters extracted from *The Rites*: "The Great Learning" and "The Doctrine of the Mean." The considered opinion of the present translator is that of the whole canon of classics only the *Lun yü*—*The Sayings of Confucius*—has something practical to say to modern Western man.

It should be noted that the classics form only one of the four traditional divisions of literature in China. The other three are histories of all types, philosophy plus religion together with specialized arts and crafts, and *belles lettres* (poetry, essays, and letters). The whole forms a most impressive literature, comparable with that of France, Germany, or England.

By nature the Chinese conceives of every organization as a patriarchy. For him all human arts and institutions have some "ancestor" as initial progenitor, and to that ancestor is felt a profound debt of gratitude. He does not know specifically where that dead ancestor may be, nor does he particularly concern himself with the problem. But at stated intervals it is customary to congregate and make public display of this gratitude through speeches, burnt offerings, hymns of praise, incense, and deep bows. Buildings similar to but more pretentious than homes have been erected as places of assembly and as the depositories of a symbol of the "ancestor." In the case of Confucius and his more famous disciples, this symbol is a mere plaque on which is written the name and title of the individual. It must be clearly understood that the Chinese have never worshiped Confucius, nor have they ever prayed to him for anything. But they have truthfully recognized him as a human being, a man, the first ancestor of the religious and literary tradition which has characterized official China historically down to and even since 1912. In the Western and in other Oriental traditions there is absolutely nothing comparable.

One of the doctrines preached in ancient China was a rigorous legalism. It held that government needed only unflinching application of a predetermined set of rules and regulations with prescribed penalties for violations. If there were no exceptions and adjustments to individual interests and interferences, all of society would run smoothly like a well-oiled machine. To this school is attributed the efficient management within the ancient state of Ch'in which enabled it to absorb gradually into itself by conquest and intrigue all the other states of China and to found the Chinese empire in 221 B.C. At the same time, the fact that this new empire remained in the hands of the founder's family for only fifteen years is eloquent evidence that its rule was inspired by priniciples which found no acceptance in the body politic. Once the nation was organized under a central capital, there appeared throughout the land men ready to express their disagreement with the unnatural principles of legalism. The death of the actual founder of the empire, The First Emperor (of China), gave the signal for revolt—an uprising which ended eventually in the founding of the Han dynasty in 202 B.C. This dynasty took some fifty years to consolidate the recently established empire, and it lasted until A.D. 220.

As the empire took form under the Han, China experienced a return to normalcy. Rejecting all the theories of the preceding centuries, she turned to the principles and practices which her teachers had been modestly transmitting to each generation of students—principles and practices noted for their sobriety and long tried in the school of human experience. It was to this segment of society that the government was forced to turn in order to build the elaborate bureaucracy without which the organization and control of the empire would have been impossible. It was this group then, rooted in the tried ways of the country, which could see its final success and victory as due to the man of Lu, Confucius, from whom all the teachers of the good old ways were, so to speak, descended. Inevitably, he was reverenced as their grand ancestor, and all doctrines and writings associated with him were accorded the same reverence. They soon stiffened into an orthodoxy. And from that day down to the present century Chinese officials have recognized their first debt of reverence to Confucius, even though they have also found it interesting and diverting to study Taoism, Buddhism, and Christianity. But the touchstone of excellence has always remained the classical tradition, in accordance with which practically all Chinese thinking and writing has been effected, for Confucius is

The Teacher-Standard of All Eternity (*Wan-shih shih-piao*).

Buddhism was first introduced into China in the first century B.C., and it gradually found widespread acceptance, but the reverence for Confucius never diminished. Through the centuries the scholar-administrators continued to give expression to their analyses of man and the universe in words and figures drawn from the old classics, even though the ideas they tried to express were clearly inspired by the abstractions characteristic of Buddhist philosophy. Eventually there gradually developed a more analytical presentation of orthodoxy which we know as Neo-Confucianism.

Not long after the discovery of the sea route around the Cape of Good Hope, Christian missionaries began to go to China, and Europe soon came to know more about China and Confucianism from the writings of the missionaries. The wave of humanism and rationalism which swept intellectual Europe in the seventeenth and eighteenth centuries appears to have derived in part from this new knowledge. A summary description of the good effects of Confucius upon Leibniz (1646-1716), Voltaire (1694-1778), and many others can be read in Professor Creel's *Confucius* (published in 1949).

But what of Confucius in China today? And what are the prospects for his continued sway over the minds of intellectuals in the China of tomorrow? One must remember that Confucius, as a person, could be the revered ancestor of the intellectual and the learned class only. China has always been a class society, a patriarchal society. In such a society the upper classes are keenly conscious of an innate obligation toward their social inferiors, and the inferiors look up to their superiors for models of good conduct and right action. Thus it can be claimed that by direct imitation and by a societal osmosis the practical aspects of high moral standards of Confucianism were transmitted down to the very depths of China's masses, although ninety percent of the population may well not have known his name. No doubt Confucius, as a person and as represented in the written tradition, is suffering an eclipse in Communist China because he is associated with those classes whose wealth is being proscribed as sops to bait the allegiance of the masses to the new political group. As students of history know, new political groups everywhere and throughout history have always proceeded thus. But the revolution, the period of anarchy, never lasts forever, because there is always present a yearning for peace and normalcy. The new regime, too, wishes to consolidate its power and enjoy a steady, predictable income. To this end China will be modernized and industrialized, but the chances are that the type of industrial reorganization will be unlike any politico-economic structure in evidence today. Industrialization, to date, has been a Western phenomenon, and it has tended toward restlessness, changes, and expansion. China, on the other hand, is historically characterized by a stronger economic steadiness and the long, long view. We might guess, for example, that she will be successful in marrying handicraft and individual artistic expression to the machine. If she does, there is a strong possibility that she will again turn to pay renewed reverence to the man who, at the beginning of a period of anarchy, 2,500 years ago, inspired confidence in China's traditional good customs and wise moral standards. Confucius will, one day, return to be acknowledged nationally as the symbol of social stability and national decorum. The teaching of such a compendium as this *Lun yü* could again instill good conduct and social harmony among China's rising citizenry.

This new translation of the *Lun yü* was undertaken in order to make a rich human document accessible to the general reader. Diligent study of *The Sayings of Confucius* can help solve the profound moral problem of the West. Reading Confucius may enable us to restate our own traditional religious beliefs and help us to realize again the value of emotion and idealism to all men.

The present volume offers a complete, unabridged translation of one whole Chinese canonical book—a work which is fundamental because every generation of students in China learned it by rote for more than two thousand years. Reading it will enable us to see humanism and rationalism expressed against a background free of all emotional involvement and characterized by that bare simplicity which is natively Chinese. To some the form may seem naive at first, but they will soon recognize the supreme virtues of clarity, simplicity, and neatness. The oldest Chinese traditions have held this book to be a selection of the sayings of Confucius and his early followers, and it does represent all that we have from the Chinese sage. The other material is slight, largely apocryphal, and scattered in canonical and historical works which have in no way enjoyed the very wide circulation, study, and citation of the *Lun yü*.

The reader can here acquaint himself with the aphorisms and stories which have served as guides to moral life and courtesy in China. The virtues stressed are fundamental for China and the Far East generally; they are recognized by civilized man everywhere: the child's love for and duty toward parents (filial duty); love for and duty between brothers (fraternal duty); reliability in friendships; loyalty to superiors; the broad public interest and what is in general right (justice); codified forms of courteous and religious action (rites); mutually forming all in all something that was probably conceived as a network of paths or roads (*tao*), System; as this complex was achieved by a man or an institution, one could be recognized as (*te*) Excellent, Accomplished, Perfect, Virtuous (a virtuoso), marked by Integrity or Character; or, thinking solely in terms of man, the goal becomes Manhood-at-its-best (Superiority); and thus one becomes the Prince of Men or Great Man. The last category is difficult for the translator. The same term, *chün-tzu,* at one moment is the ideal man, Great Man, and at another it clearly indicates a specific reigning prince. And then there are those passages where we lack certainty. It is all due to Chinese political theory which assumed that the prince attained or inherited his post by mandate of Sky; accordingly he was—or ought to be—the paragon of man. The antithesis of greatness is pettiness, or *hsiao jen.*

It will be noticed that much effort is spent in defining the term which is translated quite literally as Man-at-his-best (Superiority). The sum of these definitions will form a moral code; and the word defined provides a highly useful hint to the origin of all moral codes: they result from civilized man's self-analysis of the best that is in himself. There are many correspondences between the Chinese system here outlined and our own religious tradition. Even the most peculiarly Christian element, love, will be found in this Ancient Chinese system, but firmly rooted in its natural place, the home and family. In fact one soon sees that this collection testifies to that fullness of life which is the norm of any society. Hence it is as good a textbook as any civilization ever evolved; it represents man in utter completeness.

Such, in brief outline, is what the Chinese have studied for two millenniums as the doctrine of Confucius. It invites man to continue the traditional religious practices, for by them he is able to propitiate and control to a degree the forces of nature and they make it possible to co-operate with and abet the processes of nature. Study of the doctrine leads a man to rectify himself if he would achieve the high moral ideal. It teaches man to see himself correctly as the descendant of a long ancestry to which he owes respect and gratitude for his temporary gift of personal existence, and it teaches him that he is under obligation to see that human life continues. In short, here is humanism and rationalism in all naturalness. It should be a welcome complement and antidote to the supernaturalism of our own tradition.

Chinese words are transliterated here according to the long-established Wade-Giles system. Any consonant or group of consonants followed by an apostrophe is to be pronounced approximately as in English; the apostrophe is merely indicative of this fact. The other consonants roughly approximate these English sounds: ch is approximately j, t is d, ts is dz, and j and ih are approximately r. In Chinese personal names the surname or family name is given first: Yu Jo is Mr. Yu, Tuan-mu Tz'u is Mr. Tuan-mu, K'ung Ch'iu (Confucius) is Mr. K'ung. The rest of the name corresponds to our first names.

The term "Master"—to be understood in the sense of the French *maître*—refers of course to Confucius. I have translated *t'ien* as Sky because in Confucianism it signifies no more than that; it is neither an abode nor a paradise. *Chün-tzu* is here translated as Great Man and is the opposite of Petty Man. The new translations for *tao* and *te* I have attempted to justify above.

Chinese is basically a monosyllabic language; there is no gender, except that provided by nature; and there is neither number nor inflection nor tenses. Except for the etymologist and semanticist, there is no word-formation. Chinese is the barest and simplest of all languages. Therein lie the difficulties.

Also keep in mind: Every quotation in this book which is not attributed directly or by context to another is to be assigned to Confucius. Most of the names are those of pupils or princes. For all practical purposes the reader could substitute X, Y, or Z. The chapter titles are those used by the Chinese; they are derived from the initial statements (*incipits*) of each chapter.

CHAPTER I

As one learns . . .

1

"How pleasant it is to repeat constantly what we are learning!

"How happy we are when some friend returns from a long trip!

"To remain unconcerned though others do not know of us—that is to be Great Man!"

2

Yu Jo has said, "The filial and fraternal who are fond of offending their superiors are indeed few. Those who bring confusion to our midst always begin by being fond of offending their superiors.

"Great Man applies himself to the fundamentals, for once the fundamentals are there System comes into being. It is filial duty and fraternal duty that are fundamental to Manhood-at-its-best."

3

"Clever talk and a domineering manner have little to do with being man-at-his-best."

4

Tseng Ts'an once said, "Daily I examine myself on three points: Have I failed to be loyal in my work for others? Have I been false with my friends? Have I failed to pass on that which I was taught?"

5

"If you would bring a medium-sized state into System be sincere as you respectfully attend to your duties; while being frugal, love your fellow-men; work the people only at the proper seasons."

6

"Let youth practice filial duty; let it practice fraternal duty; let it earnestly give itself to being reliable. As it feels an affection for all let it be particularly fond of Manhood-at-its-best. Any surplus energy may be used for book-learning."

7

Pu Shang once said, "If a man adopts the proper manner in dealing with those of the highest caliber, if he can use up every ounce of energy in serving his parents, if he can go so far as to sacrifice himself in the service of his prince, if he is reliable in his relations with friends, although he is said to be uneducated, I would certainly claim that he is."

8

"If the prince is not grave he will not inspire awe; he will not abide by his studies. Let him put loyalty and reliability first, having no friend who is not like himself. If he has faults, let him not object to changing."

9

Tseng Ts'an once said, "If there is careful attention to burial rites, if the offerings are made to the dead, the people, I promise you, will turn fully to Excellence."

10

Ch'en K'ang once asked Tuan-mu Tz'u, "When our Master arrives in a place he always learns about its administration. Does he demand this information or is it given to him?"

"Our Master gets it through his gentleness, his superiority, his humility, his restraint, his complaisance. How differently from others does our Master seek his information!"

11

"While his father lives, observe a man's purposes; when the father dies, observe his actions. If for the three years [of mourning] a man does not change from the ways of his father, he may be called filial."

12

Yu Jo once said, "In carrying out the rites it is fittingness that is prized. This is what is so fine in the ways of our early kings; in all affairs, whether great or small, they followed this principle. But there is one thing which may not be allowed. To practice the principle of fittingness without subjecting it to the restraints of the rites is not allowed."

13

Yu Jo has also said, "If the maintenance of reliability does not violate justice, any promise made may be kept. If the humility that is shown does not violate the rites, there will be no shame or dishonor involved. If the reliance that is placed does not violate the interest of the family, it may be honored."

14

"If the prince does not seek satiety at table or ease at home; if, intent upon his affairs and careful of his words, he turns to those who know System and rectifies himself in accordance with it, of him I will indeed say that he is fond of learning."

15

Tuan-mu Tz'u once inquired, "What would you say of the man who, though poor, does not flatter; of the man who, though rich, is not proud?"

"They are right enough, but they are not to be compared with the one who, though poor, is happy, and the one who, though rich, is fond of the rites."

"Is this what is meant when it says in *The Poems*, 'He looks like something cut out, then filed; like something carved, then polished'?"

"With you I can at last discuss *The Poems*. When I have told you what precedes, you know what follows."

16

"I am not concerned that a man does not know of me; I am concerned that I do not know of him."

CHAPTER II

To govern . . .

1

"To be Excellent when engaged in administration is to be like the North Star. As it remains in its one position, all the other stars surround it."

2

"*The Poems*, all three hundred of them, may be summed up in one of their phrases: 'Let our thoughts be correct.'"

3

"If the people are kept in System by administration and are all treated as equals in the matter of punishment, they may succeed in doing no wrong, but they will also feel no sense of shame. On the other hand, if they are kept in System by Excellence and are treated as equals before the rites, they will reform themselves through a sense of shame."

4

"At fifteen I thought only of study; at thirty I began playing my rôle; at forty I was sure of myself; at fifty I was conscious of my position in the universe; at sixty I was no longer argumentative; and now at seventy I can follow my heart's desire without violating custom."

5

Chung-sun Ho-chi asked about filial duty.
"It consists in contravening none of the precepts."
Later, the Master said to Fan Hsü, "When asked about

filial duty I replied that it consisted in contravening none of the precepts."

"What did you mean by that?"

"While the parents live, serve them according to the rites. When they die, bury them according to the rites and make the offerings to them according to the rites."

6

When Chung-sun Chih asked about filial duty the reply came, "Let the sole worry of your parents be that you might become ill."

7

Yen Yen asked about filial duty.

"Today when people call a man filial they mean that he is supporting his parents. But he does as much for his dogs and horses! If he does not show respect for his parents, how is he differentiating between them and the animals?"

8

To Pu Shang's question on filial duty the reply was given, "Manner presents the difficulty. The mere assumption of burdens and the mere allowing of elders to be the first to eat or drink do not constitute filial duty."

9

"I can talk with Yen Hui all day, and in offering me no objections he looks like a dunce. But we find upon examination that his private life exemplifies System. Yen Hui is no dunce."

10

"Look at the means which a man employs; consider his motives; observe his pleasures. A man simply cannot conceal himself!"

11

"If, while being a student of the past, a man also understands the new things which surround us, he may be used as a teacher."

12

"Great Man is no robot."

13

Tuan-mu Tz'u asked about Great Man.
"First he sets the good example, then he invites others
to follow it."

14

"Great Man, being universal in his outlook, is impartial;
Petty Man, being partial, is not universal in outlook."

15

"Learning without thought brings ensnarement. Thought
without learning totters."

16

"It is indeed harmful to come under the sway of utterly
new and strange doctrines."

17

"Shall I tell you what knowledge is? It is to know both
what one knows and what one does not know."

18

Chuan-sun Shih studied with a view to good pay.
"After learning as much as possible and setting aside all
that is doubtful, speak circumspectly about the rest; then
you will be free from error. After seeing as much as possible and setting aside all that is not sound, carefully put
the rest into operation; then you will be free from regrets.
Let your language be free from error and your actions free
from regrets: therein lies good pay."

19

Duke Ai inquired, "What shall I do that the people may
be submissive?"

"If you employ upright officials in place of the crooked ones, the people will become submissive. If you employ crooked officials in place of the upright, your people will not be submissive."

20

Chi-sun Fei inquired how to get the people to work hard and at the same time remain respectful and loyal.

"If one is sedate in their presence, they will be respectful. If one is filial and kind, they will be loyal. If one employs the competent as officials and instructs the less able, the people will work hard."

21

Somebody once remarked to Confucius, "Why aren't you working in the government?"

"It is said in *The Writings of Old*, 'Filial duty! Just let there be filial duty! Then there will be kindliness toward brothers, and this in turn will spread to the administration.' This too is to be working in the government. Why must one actually hold office in order to work in the government?"

22

"A man who lacks reliability is utterly useless. How can we move a large vehicle which lacks its crossbar, or even a small vehicle without its crossbar?"

23

Chuan-sun Shih inquired whether it was possible to know about things ten generations from now.

"Yin succeeded to the Hsia rites, and it can be known what changes were made. Chou succeeded to the Yin, and it can be known what changes were made. If there are any successors to the Chou, even one hundred generations hence, it is possible by analogy to know their characteristics."

24

"It is flattery to make offerings to the dead who do not belong to your own family. It is cowardice to fail to do what is right."

CHAPTER III

Eight rows . . .

1

Confucius said of the Chis who used eight rows of eight singers and dancers each at the celebrations in honor of their family—only the king should use so many—that if they could permit themselves this, they were capable of anything.

2

The three great families of Lu were using a royal hymn to accompany the clearing away of the ritual utensils. "The words of the hymn go like this. 'Only princes have acted as assistants to our service, The Son of Sky has been majestic.' How do they dare use such words in the home of the three great families?"

3

"If one is not Man-at-his-best, what is the use of knowing the rites? What is the use of knowing about music?"

4

Lin Fang asked what was fundamental in the rites.

"A very important question! If in carrying out a provision of the rites you tend to be sumptuous, it would be better to cut down a bit. If in conducting your funerals you tend to take things for granted, it would be better to exhibit more grief."

5

"China without a recognized leader is preferable to foreigners with all their leaders."

6

When the Chis, who lacked the proper authority, offered sacrifice to Mt. T'ai, the Master said to their chief minister, Jan Ch'iu, "Couldn't you prevent them from violating the code?"

"No."

"Would anybody claim that Mt. T'ai is less intelligent than Lin Fang in regard to the rites?"

7

"There is nothing which Great Man will contest with others. Since it is obligatory, however, he will engage in the archery tournaments. After greeting and deferring to the others, he mounts to the range. After he has finished he comes back and plays his proper rôle in the drinking [the loser must drink; for the winner there is no compulsion]. In such a contest he is still Great Man."

8

Pu Shang asked the meaning of the following lines from *The Poems*: "Her artful smile is lovely, Her fair eyes flash black and white, To the plain and natural there is added decoration."

"Ornament is added to the plain and natural background."

"The learning of the code of rites comes only after preliminary preparation?"

"Pu Shang knows how to make my meaning clear. I can talk to him now about *The Poems*."

9

"As an expert in such matters, I can talk about the rites of the Hsia and Yin dynasties, but their descendants in Ch'i and Sung cannot prove what I say. This is because both written and oral traditions are too fragmentary. If they were not so fragmentary I should be able to prove my words, for I am a descendant of the Yin kings."

10

"At the grand sacrificial service held every five years, once the libations have been poured I no longer desire to look on, for the whole affair becomes too elaborate and confusing."

11

Some one asked for an explanation of this same grand sacrificial service.

"I cannot give one. Any person who would know how to explain it would have the world right here." And he pointed to the palm of his hand.

12

There is a dictum: Make your offerings to the ancestors as though they were actually present in person; make your offerings to the divinities as though they were actually present in person. "If I do not participate in the service, for me there has been no service."

13

Wang-sun Chia asked, "What would you say of the adage: Better to be on good terms with the spirit of the hearth, which cooks our food, than with the tutelary spirits, whom we never see?"

"I disagree. Whoever offends Sky has no court of appeal."

14

"Thanks to the two predecessors, outstanding is the culture of Chou! I follow it rather than its predecessors."

15

Whenever the Master was present at the state sacrifices to the prince's ancestors, he would inquire carefully into all that went on. This caused someone to say, "How can it be claimed that Confucius knows the rites? Every time he is present he asks about everything!" When this was reported to the Master he remarked, "Such procedure is required by the rites."

16

"In the archery contest no special emphasis is laid upon
piercing the target, for the strength of the contestants
varies. It is style that is important; such was the way of the
ancients."

17

Tuan-mu Tz'u wished to drop the custom of sacrificing a
sheep to announce to ancestors the beginning of each new
month.

"You are in love with the sheep; I, with the ceremony."

18

"If a prince were served with all due ceremony today,
people would think he was being flattered."

19

Duke Ting inquired how a prince employs his subjects
and how his subjects serve their prince.

"The prince is ceremonious; subjects, loyal."

20

"The poem *Kuan-chü* expresses joy but it is not lewd; it
expresses grief but not laceration."

21

When Duke Ai asked Tsai Yü about the altar to be
erected in honor of Earth, he replied, "The Hsias planted
pines there; the Yin, cedars; the Chou, chestnut trees. In
the last case it is said that it was to inspire the people with
fear and trembling." [Chestnut was homophonous with fear
and trembling.] When this was reported to the Master he
said, "No explanations should be offered for a thing that
is over; no objections, to a matter that is already in progress; no blame, for errors that have been committed."

22

"Kuan Chung was a man of slight ability."
Someone asked, "Was it because he was a miser?"

"He had three wives and in his household no one had double duties. How could it be due to miserliness?"

"Was Kuan Chung then well acquainted with the rites?"

"Princes of states erect screens before the entrances to their palaces, so Kuan Chung erected one too. When two princes of states have a friendly meeting they use a special serving table on which they turn their cups upside down after the drinking; Kuan Chung also had one. If one could act like Kuan Chung and still be considered to know the rites, then every one knows them!"

23

The Master spoke as follows regarding music to the Grand Maestro of Lu: "Music is simple enough. First the instruments are tuned. Then the piece is played to completion in harmony, the notes all clear, and without interruption."

24

In Yi a frontier guard seeking an interview said, "Whenever Great Man comes here I never fail to have a visit with him." The followers conducted him to Confucius, and when he came out he said, "Why are you distressed at the straits you are in? The world has been in ignorance of System for a long time; but Sky is going to use your master as a baton with which to strike the bell summoning men to instruction."

25

The Master said that Shun's music was beautiful in all respects; that it was technically perfect. He further said that the music of the founder of the Chou dynasty was beautiful in all respects, but not technically perfect.

26

"I cannot stand the sight of an overseer who is not indulgent; of a ceremonious act which is not carried out respectfully; of failure to show grief at a funeral."

CHAPTER IV

To live among the excellent . . .

1

"To live in the company of Men-at-their-best is the finest thing possible. How can a man be considered wise if, when he has the choice, he does not live in such surroundings?"

2

"Those who are not Men-at-their-best cannot stand misfortune for a long time; they cannot stand prosperity for a long time. Those who are Men-at-their-best are content with Manhood-at-its-best; the wise profit from Manhood-at-its-best."

3

"He who is solely Manhood-at-its-best will know which men to like and which ones to hate."

4

"If you are only halfheartedly bent upon being Man-at-his-best, you will hate no one."

5

"Wealth and honors are what men desire; but if they come undeserved, don't keep them. Poverty and low estate are what men dislike; but if they come undeserved, don't flee them. If Great Man avoids Manhood-at-its-best, how can we call him such? Great Man does not flee Manhood-at-its-best even for the duration of a meal. Even in haste he must abide by it; even in the direst straits he must abide by it."

6

"I have yet to meet a man fond of living Manhood-at-its-best or a man who disliked a lower degree of manhood. The one fond of living Manhood-at-its-best would prefer nothing else to it. The one who disliked a lower degree of manhood would be living Manhood-at-its-best; he would not let appear in his person anything that was not Manhood-at-its-best. Is anyone able for one day to give all his energies to living Manhood-at-its-best? I have never seen anyone who lacked the necessary energy. Perhaps there is someone so weak, but I have never met him."

7

"Men's excesses depend upon the class to which they belong. By observing his excesses we can tell whether a man is living Manhood-at-its-best."

8

"If you have learned about System in the morning, you may let yourself die that same evening."

9

"I cannot discuss things with a gentleman who, while devoted to System, is at the same time ashamed of poor clothes or bad food."

10

"Great Man's attitude toward the world is such that he shows no preferences; but he is prejudiced in favor of justice."

11

"Great Man cherishes Excellence; Petty Man, his own comfort. Great Man cherishes the rules and regulations; Petty Man, special favors."

12

"He who engages solely in self-interested actions will make himself many enemies."

13

"He who knows how to administer his state with ceremony and deference will experience no difficulties. If he does not know, he may as well dispense with rites."

14

"Do not worry about not holding high position; worry rather about playing your proper rôle. Worry not that no one knows of you; seek to be worth knowing."

15

"Tseng Ts'an, my doctrine is strung upon one single thing."

"I agree."

When the Master left someone asked, "What did he mean?"

"The Master's doctrine consists solely of loyalty and reciprocity."

16

"Great Man is conscious only of justice; Petty Man, only of self-interest."

17

"When you see a man of the highest caliber, give thought to attaining his stature. When you see one who is not, go home and conduct a self-examination."

18

"As you serve your parents you should remonstrate with them only slightly. If on doing so you find that they are set in having their own way, be even more respectful and do not thwart them. Even though this overwhelm you with toil, do not become angry with them."

19

"While your parents live, do not wander far. Let your sojourning be only in specified places."

20

"If for the three years [of mourning] one does not change from the ways of the father, one may be called filial."

21

"The parents' ages must always be known, both as a source of joy and as a source of dread."

22

"The ancients never exaggerated, for fear they themselves would not live up to the lofty sentiments."

23

"When strict with oneself one rarely fails."

24

"Great Man seeks to be slow of speech but quick of action."

25

"Excellence does not remain alone; it is sure to attract neighbors."

26

"In serving a prince rashness brings disgrace; among friends, estrangement."

CHAPTER V

Kung-yeh Ch'ang . . .

1

The Master said of Kung-yeh Ch'ang that he would make a good husband; it was not his fault that he had been in prison. So he gave him his daughter in marriage.

2

Of Nan-kung Kua he said that while System existed in the realm he would be in the government service; if System disappeared from the realm he would not be one of those to suffer. So he gave him his elder brother's daughter in marriage.

3

Of Mi Pu-ch'i the Master said, "Great Man is just like this! There must be Great Man here in our state of Lu, otherwise how would this man have become as he is?"

4

Tuan-mu Tz'u asked, "How would you characterize me?"

"A utensil."

"Which kind?"

"A fine cauldron such as was used by the ancients in their ancestral temples."

5

Somebody remarked, "Jan Yung may be Man-at-his-best but he lacks eloquence."

"Of what use is eloquence? He who engages in fluency of words to control men often finds himself hated by them. I don't know whether Jan Yung is Man-at-his-best, but of what good would eloquence be to him?"

6

The Master wanted Ch'i-tiao K'ai to take office, but he replied, "I do not yet command sufficient confidence for that." And the Master was pleased.

7

"System is not now in operation. If I were, therefore, to mount a raft and float out to sea to escape it all, Chung Yu would certainly be the one to accompany me!" And when Chung Yu heard of this he was delighted, but the Master remarked, "Chung Yu is braver than I, but I can't use him."

8

Chung-sun Chih inquired whether Chung Yu was Man-at-his-best.

"I don't know."

He asked again.

"Chung Yu could be put in charge of the military forces of a medium-sized state, but I do not know whether he is Man-at-his-best."

"What about Jan Ch'iu?"

"He could administer a small town or a small military establishment, but I do not know whether he is Man-at-his-best."

"What about Kung-hsi Ch'ih?"

"When dressed in formal garb and at court he can be used to carry on conversation with the guests, but I do not know whether he is Man-at-his-best."

9

"Who is the better, you, Tuan-mu Tz'u, or Yen Hui?"

"How can I be compared with Yen Hui? On being taught one tenth of a thing he learns all of it, while I learn only one fifth."

"No, you are not as good as he. You and I both are not as good as he!"

10

Tsai Yü stayed abed even in the daytime.

"Rotten wood may not be carved, nor a wall of manure or dirt plastered."

"What have you suffered from your contacts with Tsai Yü?"

"Formerly my attitude toward others was this: Having listened to their words, I felt I knew what their actions would be. Today my attitude is this: After listening to their words, I watch to see what their actions will be. This change is due to my contacts with Tsai Yü."

11

"I have yet to meet a steadfast person."

"There's Shen Ch'ang!"

"Shen Ch'ang is covetous, so how can we call him steadfast?"

12

Tuan-mu Tz'u said, "What I do not wish others to do unto me I also wish not to do unto others."

"You're not up to that!"

13

Tuan-mu Tz'u said, "We can be taught the external trappings of the Master; we cannot be taught the spirit of his words or his genius."

14

When Chung Yu was taught something but had not yet been able to put it into practice, his sole fear was that the experience would be repeated.

15

Tuan-mu Tz'u inquired why K'ung Yü was given the epithet of Cultured.

"He was diligent and fond of learning, and he did not blush to learn from his inferiors. That is why he was called Cultured."

16

"Kung-sun Ch'iao possessed four virtues characteristic of Great Man: humility, respect for superiors, graciousness toward dependents, and a sense of justice toward subordinates."

17

"Yen Ying is skilled in human relations; even after long acquaintance he is respectful toward others."

18

"Tsang-sun Ch'en, to keep the grand tortoise from Ts'ai, built a shelter where the capitals of the columns were carved with mountains and the beams painted with reeds. Have you ever seen such ignorance?"

19

Chuan-sun Shih said, "Prime Minister Tou Ku was three times appointed to that position but gave no sign of joy, and three times he was removed from office without a sign of sadness. Each time he told the new prime minister about the business of state. How would you characterize him?"

"He was indeed loyal."

"He was indeed Man-at-his-best, was he not?"

"I have not yet heard of anything that would warrant that assertion."

"When Ts'ui Chu slew the Prince of Ch'i, Ch'en Hsü-wu avoided him by quitting Ch'i with his ten teams of horses. When he arrived in another realm he remarked, 'The officials here are like Ts'ui Chu,' and he avoided them. This happened in every state he came to. How would you characterize him?"

"He was indeed scrupulous."

"He was Man-at-his-best, was he not?"

"I have not yet heard of anything that would warrant that assertion."

20

Chi-sun Hsing-fu acted only after thinking thrice.

"Twice is quite enough."

21

"Ning Yü displayed his wisdom while the country followed System, but when it did not, he acted stupid. His wisdom is achievable by others, his stupidity is not."

22

When in Ch'en the Master said, "Let me return! Let me return home! The pupils I left there are proving foolhardy and careless. Most elegantly are they carrying out their ornamentation, but they don't know how to fit it."

23

"Po-i and Shu-ch'i were never mindful of wrongs done to them, hence they had few enemies."

24

"No one calls Wei-sheng Kao upright! When someone asked for vinegar he sought it from a neighbor and gave it to him."

25

"Tso Ch'iu-ming was ashamed of clever talk, domineering manner, and overdeference, and I am ashamed of them too. He was also ashamed to act friendly toward a man while inwardly angry with him, and so am I."

26

Once when Yen Hui and Chung Yu were with him, the Master said, "Why don't you each tell me what you desire most?"

Chung Yu said, "I desire carriages, horses, clothes, and furs in such abundance that I could share them with my friends, and if they were damaged I would not be angry."

Yen Hui replied, "I should like never to boast of my abilities nor let my good deeds be known."

Chung Yu then said, "I should like to learn what the Master desires most."

"I should like to bring security to the aged, to be loyal to my friends, to be affectionate with the young."

27

"This is certainly the limit! I have yet to meet a man who, on observing his own faults, blamed himself!"

28

"A hamlet of ten homes will surely contain someone as loyal and reliable as I, but none to equal my love of learning."

CHAPTER VI

Jan Yung . . .

1, 2

"Jan Yung would make a good king."

Jan Yung then asked Confucius' opinion of Kung-sun Chih.

"He is adequate but simple."

"To rule simply while remaining personally respectful is certainly to be approved. Yet simple action accompanied by personal simplicity would be carrying simplicity too far."

"What Jan Yung says is correct."

3

Duke Ai asked which of the pupils was fondest of learning.

"There was Yen Hui. He was fond of learning. He never turned to anger; he never made the same mistake twice. Unfortunately he was short-lived and died. Today there are no Yen Huis. I never hear of anyone who is fond of learning."

4

While Kung-hsi Ch'ih was on a mission to Ch'i, Jan Ch'iu sought grain for his mother. The Master said, "Give her a peck." When he asked for more, the Master said, "Give her a bushel." What Jan Ch'iu gave her was a barrelful. The Master than remarked, "Kung-hsi Ch'ih went to Ch'i drawn by sleek horses and clad in fine garments, and

I have always understood Great Man does everything possible to help the poor but nothing to enrich the rich."

5

When Yüan Hsien was administrator he declined his salary of grain.

"Don't act that way! Better to take it and give it to your neighbors!"

6

To Jan Yung: "Although we may not wish to use in sacrifice the brindled cow's calf which is red and has horns, the divinities of the mountains and rivers would not reject it!"

7

"Yen Hui for three months at a time is able to think of doing nothing contrary to Manhood-at-its-best. The rest of my pupils are able to do this for but a day or a month."

8

Chi-sun Fei inquired whether Chung Yu could be employed in the government.

"Chung Yu does not hesitate to make decisions, so there is no reason why he should not be employed in the government."

Upon further inquiry the Master replied, "Tuan-mu Tz'u would be acceptable because he has known success; Jan Ch'iu, because he is talented."

9

The Chis sent a message placing Min Sun in charge of Pi, but he said to the messenger, "You will know how to decline it for me. If you return here to offer me the position again, you will certainly find me on the bank of the Wen on my way out of the state."

10

When Jan Keng was ill the Master went to visit him, but he could only grasp his hand through a window.

"We are losing him. It's indeed fate, isn't it, that such a man should be so sick? That such a man should be so sick!"

11

"Yen Hui was man of the highest caliber! With a handful of rice and a gourdful of water he dwelt in an alley. Another could not have stood the sad state Yen Hui was in; but he was always happy. I insist that he was a man of the highest caliber!"

12

Jan Ch'iu remarked, "It isn't that I dislike the Master's doctrine. It's just that I haven't enough strength to follow it."

"One who hasn't enough strength becomes exhausted in the middle of the course, but yours is a case of deliberate choice."

13

"Be Great Man among scholars, Pu Shang! Don't be Petty Man among scholars!"

14

When Yen Yen was in charge of Wu, the Master inquired, "Have you found anyone there that you can trust?"

"There's a man by the name of T'an-t'ai Mieh-ming. He is not evasive, and he has been to see me only on matters involving the public interest."

15

"Meng Ts'e is not a boaster. In the flight from the enemy he brought up the rear. But as his men were about to enter the gateway of their own city he put the whip to his horses and said, 'It isn't that I was brave enough to be last. My horses were slow.'"

16

"Even though one possesses the beauty of Ch'ao of the state of Sung, without the eloquence of prayer-leader T'o it is difficult to avoid disaster these days."

17

"Why does no one follow this doctrine of mine just as naturally as they leave a place by the door?"

18

"When substance overbalances refinement, crudeness results. When refinement overbalances substance, there is superficiality. When refinement and substance are balanced one has Great Man."

19

"Man's life span depends upon his uprightness. He who goes on living without it escapes disaster only by good fortune."

20

"Being fond of System is better than merely knowing it. Taking one's delight in it is better than merely being fond of it."

21

"With the portion of mankind that is above average one may speak of the higher things; with those below it, one may not."

22

When Fan Hsü asked for a definition of wisdom the Master replied, "If a man encourages the people to apply themselves to justice, if he respects the spirits of the departed and the divinities but is not too familiar with them, we can say that he is wise."

When he asked about Manhood-at-its-best the reply came, "He who concentrates upon the task and forgets about reward may be called Man-at-his-best."

23

"The wise take delight in water; Manhood-at-its-best delights in mountains. The wise are active; Manhood-at-its-best is quiet. The wise find enjoyment; Manhood-at-its-best enjoys a full span of life."

24

"If Ch'i but changed its ruler, it could attain to the excellence of our state of Lu. By a similar change Lu could attain System."

25

"If an urn lacks the characteristics of an urn, how can we call it an urn?"

26

Tsai Yü asked, "If one who was Man-at-his-best were told that Manhood-at-its-best was in a well, would he go in after it?"

"Why should he do that? Great Man may approach a well, but he may not be trapped in it. He can be deceived; but he cannot be ensnared."

27

"Isn't it true that Great Man studies widely with a view to refinement but, keeping everything within bounds, adheres to the code of rites and thus commits no transgression?"

28

When the Master had an interview with the infamous Lady Nan-tzu, Chung Yu was displeased. But the Master took this oath: "If I committed any wrong, may Sky crush me! May it crush me!"

29

"Excellence according to the golden mean is indeed supreme. For a long time, however, few among the people have been capable of it."

30

Tuan-mu Tz'u inquired, "What would you say if someone were to spread gifts widely in order to help all of the people? Could such an individual be called Man-at-his-best?"

"How could such a thing be achieved by mere Manhood-at-its-best? The wisest of men would be required! Even the sages Yao and Shun complained on this score! I would describe Manhood-at-its-best like this: What it desires as its own rôle, it assigns to others. The success it desires for itself it causes its fellow-men to attain. Ability to draw analogies from oneself may be called the secret of Manhood-at-its-best."

CHAPTER VII

Transmit . . .

1

"I transmit but I do not create; I am sincerely fond of the ancient. I would compare myself to our Old P'eng who was fond of talking about the good old days."

2

"To take note of things in silence, to retain curiosity despite much study, never to weary of teaching others: no one surpasses me in these three things."

3

"Not to improve my Excellence, not to pass on all that I have studied, to be taught what is proper but be unable to change, to be unable to rectify my incompetencies: these are my worries."

4

When the Master was unoccupied, he was relaxed; he looked cheerful.

5

"How I have fallen! For some time now I haven't seen the Duke of Chou in my dreams."

6

"Let your will be directed to System. Place your dependence in Excellence. Let your reliance be upon Manhood-at-its-best. Pass your time in the gentlemanly pursuits."

7

"I shall always teach, even if but a pittance be offered me."

8

"I do not instruct the uninterested; I do not help those who fail to try. If I mention one corner of a subject and the pupil does not deduce therefrom the other three, I drop him."

9

When eating beside a man in mourning the Master never ate his fill.

10

On the day that he had exhibited grief at a funeral the Master did not sing.

11

"Isn't it only you and I, Yen Hui, who are capable of this: When given employment, to work; when discarded, to live quietly?"

Chung Yu then inquired, "If you were in charge of the army, whom among us would you take with you?"

"I would not take along one who, like a raving tiger or a raging torrent, would recklessly throw away his life. What is required is someone keenly conscious of responsibility, someone fond of accomplishment through orderly planning."

12

"If one could seek the higher goal through riches, I would follow that way even if it meant being a carriage driver. Since it cannot be sought thus, I will continue to follow the way of the ancients, which I love."

13

The Master was cautious in regard to three things: fastings and purifications, battles, and illness.

14

When the Master heard in Ch'i a melody ascribed to the great sage Shun, he went three months without meat. "I never thought that so fine a melody had ever been composed!"

15

Jan Ch'iu inquired, "Does the Master side with the Prince of Wei whose father is remonstrating with him over the succession?" Tuan-mu Tz'u replied, "Yes, I'll ask him." And going in he inquired, "How would you classify Po-i and Shu-ch'i, two brothers who, swayed by the obligations of filial and fraternal duty, yielded a throne to a third brother."

"They were ancient sages."

"Did they regret their action?"

"Having sought Manhood-at-its-best, they attained it. Why should they have had regrets?"

Tuan-mu Tz'u then reported to Jan Ch'iu, "The Master does not side with the prince."

16

"To eat only vegetables without meat, to drink only water, to have only one's bent arm as a pillow: there can be joy in such a life. But to become rich and honored through injustices: for me such joy may be compared to an evanescent cloud."

17

"Give me a few more years and by fifty I shall have studied the book of divination called *Changes.* Through it I may become free of large faults."

18

The Master used the pronunciation of the capital when reciting *The Poems* and *The Writings of Old,* and also when practicing the rites.

19

Shen Chu-liang inquired about Confucius, but Chung Yu could not reply.

Later the Master said to him, "Why didn't you answer: 'The Master is a man who is so emotional about his work that he forgets to eat. He is so happy in it that he forgets his worries. He doesn't know that old age is upon him.' "

20

"I wasn't born knowing what I teach you. Being fond of the past, I sought it through diligence."

21

The Master did not speak of anomalies, feats of strength, rebellions, or divinities.

22

"When three of us are walking together I am sure to have a teacher. Having noted his competencies, I imitate them; his incompetencies I avoid."

23

"Sky begat the Excellence in me. How can Hsiang T'ui harm me?"

24

"You all think that I am hiding something from you! I have no secrets! I do nothing that I do not share with you. I am that kind of person."

25

The Master taught four things: literature, conduct, loyalty, and reliability.

26

"It has not been my fortune to meet a sage, but perhaps I shall meet with Great Man. It has not been my fortune to meet a competent man, but perhaps I shall meet one possessed of constancy. But when a man pretends to possess something which he lacks; when, knowing nothing, he claims omniscience; when, being petty, he claims to be great: such a man does not possess constancy."

27

The Master fished with a hook but not with a net. He did not shoot his arrow at a sitting bird.

28

"There may be some who create things without knowledge, but I am not of that type. After being taught much I selected the best and followed it; I observed much and remembered it. This is knowledge of the second rank." [Compare XVI, 9.]

29

It was hard to converse with the people of Hu, so when a lad arrived and sought an interview with Confucius, the pupils were in a quandary.

"I do not sanction his departure just because I sanction his arrival. Why all the worry? When a man, having cleansed himself, arrives, I receive him; but I don't guarantee his future."

30

"Manhood-at-its-best is no remote ideal! We have only to desire it and straightway it arrives."

31

An official from the State of Ch'en inquired whether Duke Chao was well acquainted with the rites, and Confucius replied that he was.

Confucius having withdrawn, the official received Wuma Shih and said, "I have been taught that Great Man is impartial, but perhaps Great Man is partial after all. The Prince of Lu, Duke Chao, took as wife a woman of Wu, and since she had the same clan name as himself he called her Wu Meng-tzu in order to conceal the fact. Now if, as prince, he is considered to know the rites when he commits such violations, then everybody knows them!"

When Wu-ma Shih reported this, the Master replied, "Whenever I make a mistake people are sure to know it!"

32

Whenever the Master sang with another and found him skilled he would harmonize with him by having him repeat the song.

33

"I give the best that is in me, just as others do, but as for personifying Great Man in service to the state, that I have not yet achieved."

34

"I make no claim to be a sage or to be Manhood-at-its-best; but it can be said of me that I act unstintingly with them in view, and that I never weary of teaching others."

Upon this Kung-hsi Ch'ih spoke up, "You're right; but your pupils do not know how to imitate you."

35

When the Master fell ill Chung Yu asked him to pray, and he answered, "Are there any that can be said?"

"Yes. The eulogies read, 'In prayer we turn to the divinities above and here below.'"

"My prayer has been in progress for a long time indeed."

36

"Extravagance leads to disobedience; parsimony leads to miserliness. Of the two I prefer miserliness."

37

"Great Man is completely at ease; Petty Man is always on edge."

38

The Master was gentle in his severity. Although he inspired awe he was not brusque; although humble, he was completely at ease.

CHAPTER VIII

Count T'ai . . .

1

"Count T'ai can certainly be called a man of Excellence in its highest form. Although he three times declined the throne, he did it so quietly that the people never got around to praising him for it."

2

"Not to follow the rites in being humble is annoyance. Not to follow them in exercising care is timidity. Not to follow them in acts of bravery is confusion. Not to follow them in uprightness is rudeness.

"If the prince is faithful to his family, the people will abound in evidences of Manhood-at-its-best. If he does not neglect his old friends, the people will not be fickle."

3

When Tseng Ts'an was ill he summoned his pupils and said, "Uncover my feet! Uncover my hands! to show that I have been filial enough to preserve them intact, for *The Poems* say, 'Be fearful as though looking over a deep abyss or as though treading on thin ice.' From now on, however, I shall know how to escape disaster, shall I not, pupils?"

4

When Tseng Ts'an was on his deathbed Chung-sun Chieh visited him, and Tseng Ts'an said, "When a bird is about to die its cry is mournful, but when a man is about to die his words are practical. Now there are three things of value which Great Man draws from System: In his actions he avoids violence and disrespect; in his appearance he seeks sincerity; in the tenor of his speech he avoids vileness and vulgarity. The utensils used in the sacrifices he leaves to the care of those in charge."

5

Tseng Ts'an said, "I once had a friend, Yen Hui, who was like this: although capable he would inquire of the less competent; although he knew much he would inquire of those who knew less; his possession looked like non-possession; his fullness resembled emptiness; mistreatment he did not return."

6

Tseng Ts'an said, "He can be entrusted with the education of a young child; he can be entrusted with the rule of a state; in a moment of crisis he remains unshaken: is such a man Great Man? He is."

7

Tseng Ts'an said, "The gentleman must be brave and courageous, for his burden is heavy and his road long. Manhood-at-its-best is his personal burden, and how heavy it is! After death it is over, but how far off that is!"

8

"Stir emotions with *The Poems*. Assign proper rôles with the rites. Provide unity with music."

9

"The people can be made to follow [System], but they cannot be made to understand it."

10

"He who is fond of bravery but complains of poverty is going to create disorder.

"If the human being who is not Man-at-his-best suffers too much, disorder will ensue."

11

"Though a man possess all the good qualities of the Duke of Chou, if he is proud and miserly the rest of him does not merit consideration."

12

"It is hard to find a man who will study for three years without thinking of a post in government."

13

"In all sincerity and fidelity be fond of learning. Even if you die in its defense, become skilled in System. Do not enter a state which is tottering. Do not remain in a state which is in rebellion. If the world is following System, let yourself be seen therein; if not, live in hiding. If a state is following System, it is a disgrace to be in poverty and low estate therein; if not, it is a disgrace to be rich and honored therein."

14

"Let the other man do his job without your interfernce."

15

"When the maestro Chih took up his office, how the final strains of the poem *Kuan-chü* in all their glory filled our ears!"

16

"To be less than upright and at the same time foolhardy, to be less than diligent and at the same time immature, to be unreliable and at the same time incompetent: I have nothing to teach about such things."

17

"Study as if you were never to master it; as if in fear of losing it."

18

"How exalted was the way in which Shun and Yü ruled the world! They did so with detachment."

19

"Great was Yao as a prince! How exalted! It was the greatness of Sky that Yao took as model. How vast! The people lacked terms to describe him. How exalted were his accomplishments! How brilliant his elegance!"

20

Under Shun, five officials kept the world in order. King Wu is quoted as saying, "I have ten officials to keep order."

In this regard Confucius once said, "How true it is that talent is hard to come by! It was most abundant in the time of Yao and Shun. Under King Wu one was a woman, so there were but nine men. While in possession of two-thirds of the world to continue in submission to a depraved Yin was the Excellence of the founder of the Chou dynasty. It may be called the supreme form of Excellence."

21

"I find no fault in Yü. Although abstemious in his own consumption of food and drink, he was reverent toward the spirits and divinities. Although poor in his own dress, the vestments for the services were beautiful. While living in a humble abode, he devoted all his energies to the digging of irrigation canals. I find no fault in Yü."

CHAPTER IX

Rarely did the Master . . .

1

The Master rarely spoke of profit; his attachment was to fate and to Manhood-at-its-best.

2

A man of Ta-hsiang said, "Great indeed is Confucius! His learning is wide but there is nothing for which he is particularly renowned."

When this was reported, the Master replied to his pupils, "What is my strong point? Is it driving or is it shooting? It is driving, the humblest of the six arts."

3

"A hemp hat was required by the rites of old, but today everyone uses silk. I follow the majority. The rites require that one bow at the foot of the steps, but today everyone bows at the top, and this is presumption. Though it is contrary to the majority, I continue to bow at the foot."

4

The Master recognized four prohibitions: Do not be swayed by personal opinion; recognize no inescapable necessity; do not be stubborn; do not be self-centered.

5

When imperiled at K'uang the Master spoke as follows: "When King Wen died, did his high culture (*wen*) disappear too? If Sky had wished that this high culture come to nought, it would not have permitted a single subsequent person to have become attracted to it. Since Sky has not let it come to nought, what can the people of K'uang do to me?"

6

The Prime Minister of Wu asked Tuan-mu Tz'u, "If your master is a sage, why does he know so many trades?"

"There is no question but that Sky gave him free rein to become a sage, but he does know many trades."

When it was reported, the Master said, "The prime minister reallys knows me! As a youth I was poor, hence I learned to do many things. But does Great Man have many trades? No!"

7

Ch'in Lao remarked, "The Master used to say, 'Since I have not been employed as an official, I know how to do things.' "

8

"Am I a wise man? No! But if a lowly person asks me a question in complete ignorance, I tell him all I know about it from beginning to end."

9

"The phoenix does not arrive; the river does not produce a design. It must be deduced that this age is to have no sage-king. I am through, am I not?"

10

When the Master received a man dressed in mourning, or an official, or a blind man, even though they were younger, he would always rise. When passing them, he would do so quickly.

11

Yen Hui once heaved a long sigh and said, "When I look up at the Master's doctrine, I find it high. When I bore into it, it is hard. When I catch sight of it before me, it suddenly is behind me. But the Master is skilled in leading others forward step by step. To broaden me he uses books. To put restraints upon me he uses the rites. When I wish to give up, I find myself unable to do so. When I have given his doctrine all that is in me, there is still something unconquered, and even though I wish to pursue it, I can't."

12

When the Master was seriously ill, Chung Yu had his pupils act as his official attendants. When the illness eased, the Master said, "For a long time now Chung Yu has been deceiving me. In acting as if there were official attendants when there are none, whom do I deceive, Sky? As compared to dying in the hands of attendants, I would prefer to die in the hands of you, my pupils. Even though I would not thus have an elaborate funeral, I would not be dying as if alone by the roadside."

13

Tuan-mu Tz'u inquired, "If you had a jewel, would you keep it in a box or would you sell it for the highest price?"

"I would sell it certainly, but I would wait for the purchaser."

14

When the Master wanted to go live among the tribes somebody remarked, "What about their crudeness?"

"If Great Man were living among them, how could they be crude? His very presence would alter all that."

15

"Since I have returned from Wei to Lu the music has been corrected, and *The Poems* returned to their proper status."

16

"In public serve one's superior's and in private serve one's father and elder brothers. Be zealous in carrying out funeral arrangements. Do not come under the influence of alcohol. These are not problems for me."

17

Standing on the bank of a stream, the Master said, "Those who leave their native localities are similar, are they not? It stops neither day nor night."

18

"I have yet to meet a man as fond of Excellence as he is of outward appearances."

19

"My teaching may be compared to the building of a mountain. If a man stops before the last load is placed, I stop. It may be compared to leveling land. Even though a man but deposit one load, there is progress. I go to him."

20

"The one who can speak of my doctrine without becoming weary is Yen Hui."

21

"What a pity that Yen Hui is gone! I saw him progress, but I never found out his limit."

22

"Isn't it true that some shoots do not survive, while others survive but produce no grain?"

23

"Juniors are to be respected. How do we know that they will not be our equals in the future? If at forty or fifty, however, they have achieved no reputation, they need no longer be respected."

24

"Standard-setting directives must be followed, but the important thing is self-reformation. The words of appointment to a post are pleasing, but the important thing is self-reflection. There is nothing I can do about cases of satisfaction without self-reflection, or of compliance without self-reformation."

25

"Put loyalty and reliability first. Have no friends inferior to yourself. If you have faults do not fear self-improvement."

26

"A commander may be snatched away from his army, but will cannot be taken from the humblest man."

27

"The one who, though clad in poor clothes, can stand unabashed among those clad in furs is indeed Chung Yu. As it says in *The Poems,* 'He does no harm, he seeks nothing. What need has he of doing wrong?' "

When Chung Yu kept reciting this the Master remarked, "This is what System demands! Must you dwell upon such characteristics?"

28

"When the weather turns cold, we realize that the pines and firs are the last to fade."

29

"Wisdom has no doubts. Manhood-at-its-best has no concerns. Courage is without fear."

30

"It may be possible to study with someone without being able to approach with him to System. It may be possible to approach System with someone without being able to become established therein with him. It may be possible to become established therein with someone without being able to exercise judgment along with him.

"*The Poems* read, 'As the flowers of the cherry tree flutter and turn could I help but think of you? Yet your home is far from here.' This means that before we give it thought, a thing can seem to be near when it is not."

CHAPTER X

At home . . .

1

At home Confucius was pleasant and agreeable, but more like a person who could not express himself. At the ancestral temple or the prince's court he spoke up clearly and with facility, but always respectfully.

At court, when speaking with a grand gentleman of lesser rank he was frank and firm; with those of higher rank he was affable and discursive. When the prince was present he was respectful to the point of allowing nervousness to show; he was ceremonious to the highest degree.

2

When the prince placed him in charge of receiving visitors from another state, his countenance changed and his step became uncertain. When he bowed to the visitors, his clasped hands were turned to the left and then to the right in order to greet them in proper sequence; meanwhile, his skirt remained well adjusted both front and back. As he hurried to report the arrival to the prince, his arms extended to either side in such way as to resemble a bird's wings. When the visitors withdrew he would always report to the prince, "Your guests are no longer looking this way."

3

On entering the duke's gateway he would bow as though there were not room to remain upright. He would not stand in the doorway; he would not step on the threshold as he entered. As he passed by the prince's empty place, his countenance would change and his step become uncertain; his speech became like a dumb man's. As he mounted with lifted skirt to the audience hall he seemed to be making a bow; he held his breath as though unable to breathe. On leaving, as soon as he had descended one step, he looked pleased. From the bottom of the steps he moved quickly forward, his arms extended in such a way as to make one think of a bird's wings. On returning to his own place at the reception he became respectful to an extreme degree.

4

When on an official mission to another state, he grasped the jade tablet which served as the badge of his appointment as though he were bowing and as though it were too heavy for him to lift. He raised it as though he were making the grasped-hand salutation; he lowered it as though he were making a presentation. All of a sudden he would seem to tremble; his feet scarcely moved, as though he were following closely behind someone. He presented his prince's gifts calmly. He presented his own gifts pleasantly.

5

Great Man does not have the edge of the collar of his garments colored either plum or deep red. The garments which he wears about the house are neither red nor violet. In summer he wears about the house a single gown of either fine or coarse hemp; when leaving the house he adds an additional gown. In winter his outer black gown is worn over a gown lined with lamb's wool; the outer undyed gown is worn over one lined with deer's fur; the outer yellow gown is worn over one lined with fox fur. At home he wears a lined gown which is longer than the one he would wear on ceremonial occasions; in addition the right sleeve is kept short at home for convenience in using the arm. He always wears a nightshirt, and it is half again as long as his body. For home wear his gowns are lined with thick fox or badger fur. Except for funerals, he always wears all his insignia hanging from his sash. Except for the skirt worn at sacrifices, his clothes always are cut and fitted. On visits of condolence he wears neither the wool-lined gown nor the dark hat. On the first day of the month he always attends upon his prince dressed in formal attire. When fasting he always wears freshly laundered clothes made of hemp.

6

When he fasts his food is different from the usual fare; he also rests in a different place. For his gruel he does not object to finely ground grain; he does not object to finely chopped meats. Grain, fish, or meat which are spoiled he does not eat. He does not eat a thing whose color or odor is not right. He does not eat what is too ripe or too green. He eats nothing out of season. He does not eat what has not been properly cut. He does not eat without the proper sauce. Although the meat may be abundant he does not eat more of it than he does of the vegetables. He does not restrict the amount of his wine, but he does not let it befuddle him. He does not partake of wine and dried meats which have been purchased at a store. He does not refuse food seasoned with ginger, but he does not eat too much of it. When, having assisted his prince in a sacrifice, he receives a present of meat, he does not keep it overnight. After three days he does not eat at all the meat of a sacrifice which has been made in his own home. He does not talk with anything in his mouth. He does not talk when going to sleep. Even though it is simple food and the soup is of herbs, when offering some to the deceased he always does so respectfully.

7

If the mat is not straight he does not sit on it.

When his fellow villagers hold a feast, he leaves immediately after the elderly folk have gone.

8

When his fellow villagers are engaged in driving off the demon of pestilence, he dresses in formal attire and stands to the east at the foot of the steps leading up to the ancestral temple.

9

When he sends a messenger to inquire after someone in another state he bows deeply twice and then dismisses him.

10

When Chi-sun Fei sent him medicine he received it with a deep bow but said, "Since I do not recognize it, I will not put it to my mouth."

11

When his stable was burned the Master returned home from the palace and inquired, "Was anyone injured?" He did not ask about the horses.

12

When his prince presented him with food he always straightened his mat before sitting down to eat. If the present was raw meat he always had it cooked before offering it to his ancestors as a prelude to his own meal. When the present was a living animal he always kept it.

Whenever he had a meal with his prince, while the prince was offering food to his ancestors, the Master would be the first to taste of all the dishes as a protection to his prince.

13

When he was sick abed and his prince visited him, he would lie with his head to the east, and lay his formal gown over himself with the sash in proper position.

14

Whenever the prince summoned him to the palace he would start without waiting for his carriage to be hitched up.

15

Whenever he was present at the state sacrifices to the prince's ancestors he would inquire carefully into all that went on.

16

When a friend died homeless Confucius would say, "Entrust the funeral to me."

Presents from friends, even vehicles and horses—with the exception of meat from the sacrifices—he did not acknowledge with a deep bow.

17

He would not lie down in such a way as to resemble a corpse. When at home he lived informally.

18

On receiving a man in mourning, even though a close friend, he would assume an appropriate air. When receiving an official or a blind man, even though he knew him very well, he would assume an appropriate attitude.

If from his carriage he saw a man in mourning, he would greet him. He would also greet any one carrying the census record.

Whenever his bowl was filled at a feast he would blush and rise to thank his host.

At a sudden clap of thunder or a gust of wind he would always flush.

19

When getting into his carriage he held himself erect and grasped the rope firmly. Once in the carriage he did not peer around; he did not shout; he did not point.

20

Seeing the group, a bird flew out of reach, and after flitting about for a time came to perch. Confucius then remarked, "The female bird there on the ridge certainly knows how to adapt itself to conditions!" When Yen Yen tried to catch it, it uttered three cries and flew away.

CHAPTER XI

The pioneers . . .

1

"The first ones to have formulated the rites and music are called crude; those later, Great Men. When it is a question of drawing upon rites and music, I follow the work of the pioneers."

2

"None of those who accompanied me to Ch'en and Ts'ai got as far as the princes' gates."

3

Yen Hui, Min Sun Jan Keng, and Jan Yung were known for their Excellence; Tsai Yü and Tuan-mu Tz'u, for eloquence; Jan Ch'iu and Chung Yu, as administrators; Yen Yen and Pu Shang, for their book-learning.

4

"Yen Hui was not one to help me develop my theme; he was satisfied with everything I said."

5

"Min Sun could be called filial, for no one speaks of him any differently than his parents and brothers."

6

Because Nan-kung Kua repeated three times the line of *The Poems* stressing careful speech Confucius gave him his brother's daughter for wife.

7

When Chi-sun Fei inquired which of the pupils was fondest of learning, Confucius replied, "There was Yen Hui. He was fond of learning, but unfortunately, his life was short. Today there is no one who is fond of learning."

8

When Yen Hui died his father asked for the Master's carriage that he might exchange it for an external coffin. The Master replied, "Whether talented or not, I call all pupils 'son.' When my own son, Li, died, we used simply the one coffin and not an external one. I did not go about on foot in order to provide him with an external coffin. Further, being myself the son of a grand gentleman, it is improper for me to go about on foot."

9

When Yen Hui died the Master cried, "Alas, Sky is bringing my efforts to nought."

10

When Yen Hui died the Master wept for him bitterly, and a follower remarked, "You are weeping too bitterly."

"Not too bitterly. If I didn't weep bitterly for such a man, for whom would I weep bitterly?"

11

When Yen Hui died the other pupils wished to bury him with all possible pomp, but Confucius disapproved. Nevertheless, they did bury him with pomp, and the Master said, "Yen Hui looked upon me as a father, but I have not been successful in treating him as I did my own son. This is not my fault. It is your fault, my pupils." [*Compare No. 8, above.*]

12

Chung Yu inquired about the proper treatment of spirits and divinities.

"You cannot treat spirits and divinities properly before you are able to treat your fellow-men properly."

When he inquired about death, the reply came, "You cannot know about death before you know about life."

13

When attending the Master, Min Sun looked pleased; Chung Yu, stern; Jan Ch'iu and Tuan-mu Tz'u, frank; and the Master was pleased. But of Chung Yu he said, "He will not die a natural death."

14

When the leaders of Lu were rebuilding their treasury, Min Sun remarked, "Wouldn't it be adequate to keep the old one? Why must it be rebuilt?" And the Master said, "This man is not given to talking, but when he says something it is certain to be to the point."

15

"Why is Chung Yu playing the cither at my doorway?" Thereupon the pupils showed little respect for Chung Yu, but the Master remarked, "What I meant was that Chung Yu has indeed come to the house, but he has not yet entered my room."

16

Tuan-mu Tz'u inquired which was of the higher caliber, Chuan-sun Shih or Pu Shang. "The former is excessive; the latter, deficient."

"In that case, Chuan-sun Shih is of higher caliber."

"Excess and deficiency are equally at fault."

17

The Chis were richer than the Duke of Chou had ever been, yet Jan Ch'iu, by accumulating taxes for them, increased their wealth. Therefore, the Master declared, "He is no pupil of mine! Pupils, you have my permission to attack him with your drums rolling."

18

The pupil Kao Ch'ai was stupid. Tseng Ts'an was dull. Chuan-sun Shih was flighty. Chung Yu was coarse.

"Yen Hui almost achieved the ideal, but he was frequently penniless. Tuan-mu Tz'u did not accept fate, but made money whenever he wished."

19

When Chuan-sun Shih inquired about the characteristics of the expert, the Master replied, "He does not follow established precedent. He also does not make himself one of us."

On another occasion the Master replied to the same question, "He is given to frank and honest discourse, but is he Great Man or is he merely impressive?"

20

Chung Yu inquired whether he should put into immediate effect something which he had just learned.

"How can you do so while your father and an elder brother are still alive?"

To Jan Ch'iu's similar question the reply came, "Yes. Put it into immediate effect."

Kung-hsi Ch'ih then spoke up, "The replies which you have just given confuse me."

"Jan Ch'iu is slow, so I urged him to promptness; Chung Yu has enough energy for two, so I slowed him down."

21

When the Master was imperiled at K'uang the pupil Yen Hui had been left behind. When they were reunited the Master said, "I had given you up for dead."

"Would I dare die while you remained alive?"

22

Chi Tzu-jan inquired whether Chung Yu and Jan Ch'iu, who were in his employ, might be considered great ministers.

"I thought you were going to inquire about something

extraordinary, but you ask only about Chung Yu and Jan Ch'iu. The so-called great minister serves his prince according to System, and if that is impossible, he quits his post. I would call these two men run-of-the-mill ministers only."

"In that case, will they be obedient?"

"They will not go so far as to slay a father or a prince."

23

Chung Yu put Kao Ch'ai in charge of Pi.

"He will bring them decadence."

"There are people and altars there, which will give him practical experience. Why should he take time for studies now? He can do that later."

"This is why I dislike the talker."

24

Chung Yu, Tseng Tien, Jan Ch'iu, and Kung-hsi Ch'ih were seated in attendance.

"Forget that I am a bit older than you, and answer me frankly. As you are not employed in government you are always saying that you are unknown. Suppose that someone did employ you in government what would you do?"

Chung Yu replied hastily, "Suppose a medium-sized state were caught between two large ones and invaded by troops so that a famine ensued. If I were in charge, within three years it would have bold soldiers and also a strategy." The Master smiled at him.

"What would you do, Jan Ch'iu?"

"If I could have charge of a tiny territory for three years, I could bring its people sufficiency. For rites and music it would need to await Great Man."

"And you, Kung-hsi Ch'ih?"

"I do not consider myself ready for office, but I should like to learn through holding one. I should like to be an assistant at the ancestral sacrifices and also at the formal general meetings, as well as the daily meetings at the court."

"Tseng Tien?"

He gave a final strumming or two to his cither, and, laying it down while it was still vibrating, he replied, "I would do things differently from the other three."

"That doesn't matter. Each is merely expressing his own mind."

"Well, when spring is over and the heavier clothing put away, along with five or six young men and six or seven lads, I like to bathe in the river Yi, air myself in the rain-dance, and then return home singing."

"I would join with Tseng Tien."

When the other three left, Tseng Tien remained behind and asked, "What do you think of what the three others said?"

"Each of them was merely expressing his own mind."

"Why did you smile in the case of Chung Yu?"

"A state is to be governed through the rites, but his words showed no humility; hence I smiled at him."

"In Jan Ch'iu's case there was no question of a state."

"Did you ever see even a small territory that wasn't a state?"

"Well, then, in the case of Kung-hsi Ch'ih there was no state involved."

"Can ancestral sacrifices and formal general meetings be conducted by other than a feudal lord? Yet, if Kung-hsi Ch'ih holds the low office, who would know enough to hold the high?"

CHAPTER XII

Yen Hui . . .

1

When Yen Hui asked for a definition of Manhood-at-its-best, the Master replied, "The subduing of oneself and the return to the practice of the rites constitute Manhood-at-its best. If for one day you achieve self-control and return to the practice of the rites, the world will acknowledge you as Man-at-his-best. The achieving of Manhood-at-its-best must come from you yourself; one does not acquire it from others!"

"What are the constituent parts of self-control and the return to the rites?"

"Look at nothing which is contrary to the rites; listen to nothing contrary to them; speak nothing contrary thereto; do nothing contrary thereto."

"I am not very diligent, but this is exactly what I am going to do."

2

Jan Yung asked about Manhood-at-its-best.

"When away from home act as respectfully as you would toward an important guest; handle the people as respectfully as you would the grand sacrifice. Do not do to others what you would not desire yourself. Then you will have no enemies either in the state or in your own home."

"I am not very diligent, but this is exactly what I am going to do."

3

To Ssu-ma Li he said, "Man-at-his-best is circumspect in what he says."

"Is circumspection in speech sufficient for one to be known as Man-at-his-best?"

"What such a man is achieving is difficult, so can he help but be circumspect in speaking of it?"

4

Ssu-ma Li asked about Great Man.

"Great Man neither worries nor fears."

"Is that sufficient for one to be known as Great Man?"

"If upon self-examination one is found free from fault, what is there to worry about or to fear?"

5

Ssu-ma Li said worriedly, "All of you have brothers except me."

Pu Shang replied, "What I have been taught is this: Life and death are governed by fate, and riches and honors depend upon Sky. If Great Man is faultlessly respectful; if he is humble within the rites to his fellow men, then in the whole, wide world, all are his brothers. How can Great Man complain that he has no brothers?"

6

Chuan-sun Shih asked for a definition of intelligence.

"To be uninfluenced by slow-seeping aspersions and superficial complaints may be called intelligence; it may be called transcendence."

7

Tuan-mu Tz'u inquired about the essentials of good government.

"They are these: sufficient food, sufficient armament, and the confidence of the people."

"Suppose a necessity arose and, despite oneself, it was impossible to have all three. Which should be dispensed with first?"

"Armament."

"And if one of the remaining two had to be dispensed with?"

"Food. Everyone has always been subject to death, but without the confidence of the people there would be no government."

8

Chi Tzu-ch'eng declared, "Great Man consists solely of substance. What need has he of refinement?"

Tuan-mu Tz'u then remarked, "Unfortunate indeed is your explanation of Great Man! It has been truly said that a four-horse team cannot overtake a man's tongue. Refinement is like substance and substance like refinement in the same way that leather from the skin of the tiger or leopard resembles leather from the skin of the dog or sheep. This is true only after the hair has been removed from the hide!"

9

Duke Ai asked Yu Jo, "What is to be done when the harvest fails and our supplies are insufficient?"

"Why not levy a tax of one-tenth?"

"I find a tax of two-tenths insufficient, so how can I follow your suggestion?"

"When the people have sufficient, how can the prince fail to have enough? If the people do not have sufficient, how can the prince have enough?"

10

Chuan-sun Shih inquired about Excellence in its exalted form and about the clear understanding of utter confusion.

"Exalted Excellence is the giving of first place to loyalty and reliability and the turning to the practice of justice. Life is desired for those we love, and death for those we hate. When, however, at one and the same time we desire for them both life and death, we are in utter confusion. As *The Poems* say, 'Truly not for wealth, only indeed for difference in quality.'"

11

When Duke Ching of the state of Ch'i inquired about the characteristics of good government, the answer came, "Let the prince be as a prince. Let the minister be as a minister. Let the father be as a father. Let the son be as a son."

"Perfect! If things were not as you have just stated them, I might not succeed in eating even if there were an abundance of grain."

12

"If anyone can decide a case in a few words, it is Chung Yu. He gives assents immediately."

13

"In hearing cases I am like everyone else. The important thing, however, is to see to it that there are no cases!"

14

Chuan-sun Shih asked about government.

"Let the official give himself no respite, and let all his acts be loyal."

15

"Isn't it true that by studying widely in the books, but keeping it all within bounds by adhering to the code of rites, one will thus commit no transgression?"

16

"Great Man develops the virtues in others, not their vices. Petty Man does just the opposite."

17

Regarding government Confucius said to Chi-sun Fei, "By etymology, the one engaged in government (*cheng*) corrects and is himself correct (*cheng*). If you are all correctness in your leadership, who would dare not be likewise?"

18

Chi-sun Fei complained to Confucius about robberies. "If you yourself had no desires, people would not steal even for pay."

19

On another occasion Chi-sun Fei inquired, "Suppose I slay those who do not follow System, so that only the followers thereof are left?"

"Why do any slaying in your exercise of government? If you yourself desire competence, the people will indeed be competent. Excellence in the prince may be compared to the wind; that in the people, to the grass. When the grass is put upon by the wind, it must bend."

20

Chuan-sun Shih inquired under what conditions a gentleman could be said to have succeeded.

"What do you mean by success?"

"To have a good reputation both in the state and within one's own home."

"This is reputation; it's not success. The one who has succeeded is upright in his very substance and fond of justice. While watching his every word and facial expression, he is concerned with placing himself below others. Then both in the state and within his own home he is considered to have succeeded. The man with merely a reputation assumes the attitude of Manhood-at-its-best, but his every action belies it. Nevertheless, within himself he never doubts but that he is Man-at-his best. Thus he has a good reputation both in the state and within his own home."

21

One day when Fan Hsü was walking in the Master's suite at the site of the rain-dance he inquired about Excellence in its exalted form, amelioration of vices, and the clear understanding of utter confusion.

"What good questions! Consider your job of prime importance; put the reward in second place—wouldn't this be Excellence in its exalted form? To war against one's own bad points and not against those of others—wouldn't this be amelioration of vices? In a moment's burst of anger to forget oneself and one's family—wouldn't this be utter confusion?"

22

In answer to Fan Hsü's questions the Master said, "To love one's fellow-men is Manhood-at-its-best. To know them is to have knowledge."

Since this was not yet clear to him, the Master continued, "If you will appoint upright persons to the places now held by the crooked, you will be making the crooked straight."

Then Fan Hsü retired and reported the conversation to Pu Shang. "What did he mean?" inquired Fan Hsü.

"Rich indeed are those words of his! When Shun ruled the world, making his selection from the whole group, he elevated Kao Yao to high position, and those who were not Men-at-their-best were set aside. When T'ang the Victorious, founder of the Yin dynasty, ruled the world, he too, choosing from the whole group, elevated I Yin to high position, and those who were not Men-at-their-best were set aside."

23

To Tuan-mu Tz'u regarding friends: "In all loyalty pointing out their good and bad points, be skillful in guiding them. If they disapprove, desist. Don't go so far as to shame yourself in their eyes."

24

Tseng Ts'an once said, "Great Man uses the books to bring together friends, and through friendships he bolsters up Manhood-at-its-best."

CHAPTER XIII

Chung Yu . . .

1

To Chung Yu, on government: "Require of others only what you have first taught them."

When he asked for additional guidance he was told: "Never grow weary."

2

When Jan Yung was administrator for the Chis he asked about government.

"You must first place people in charge of various matters, then pardon any slight mistakes, and promote those of the highest caliber and those with talents."

"How shall I recognize the talented and those of the highest caliber that I may promote them?"

"Promote those that you actually know to be such. Those you do not know personally others will mention to you."

3

Chung Yu said, "If the Prince of Wei were waiting for the Master to administer his government, what would you place first on your agenda?"

"Of indispensable importance would be to render all designations accurately."

"Do you really mean that? You're getting far afield! Why would you correct them?"

"How crude Chung Yu is! I would say that Great Man

abstains from what he doesn't know. If the designations are not accurate, language will not be clear. If language is not clear, duties will not be carried out. If duties are not carried out, rites and music will not flourish. If rites and music do not flourish, then punishments will not be specific. If punishments are not specific, then the people will do nothing without getting into trouble. Hence when Great Man has given something a name it may with all certainty be expressed in language; when he expresses it, it may with certainty be set in operation. In regard to his language Great Man is never careless in any respect."

4

Fan Hsü wanted to study farming with the Master, but the latter said, "You had better see an old farmer." When the same man sought to study gardening with him: "You had better see an old gardener."

When Fan Hsü left, the Master said, "He is Petty Man. When those at the top love the rites, the people will of necessity be respectful; when justice is observed at the top, the people will be submissive; when reliability reigns at the top, the people will be sincere. Then, when such a situation prevails, people from all over will move to that place bringing their children on their backs. What good is farming?"

5

"Suppose a man is able to recite all three hundred of *The Poems,* but when he is given a position in the government he is unsuccessful. Suppose he is then sent on missions to the various states, but proves unable to think for himself. Even though he may know many poems, why continue to employ him?"

6

"If the official is himself upright, the people will play their rôles without orders. If he is not upright, even under orders the people will be disobedient."

7

"The governments of Lu and Wei may be considered brothers, since their land-holdings were founded by brothers."

8

Regarding Kung-tzu-ching of Wei: "He knows how to enjoy his home. When he first began to have things he would say, 'This is just about right.' When he had a bit more he would say, 'This is just about enough.' When he became rich he would say, 'This is just about perfection.'"

9

When the Master went to Wei, Jan Ch'iu conducted him. "What a large population!"

"Since the people are already numerous, what more would you see them have?"

"I would enrich them."

"And then?"

"I would instruct them."

10

"If some ruler would employ me, in a month I should have my system working. In three years everything would be running smoothly."

11

"If an able man were to govern a place for one hundred years, he could indeed subdue the evil and dispense with killings. This saying is certainly true!"

12

"If there were a true king upon the throne of China, unquestionably Manhood-at-its-best would prevail within one generation."

13

"If a man has rendered himself correct, he will have no trouble governing. If he cannot render himself correct, how can he correct others?" [*Compare XII, 17.*]

14

Jan Ch'iu returned from the court.

"Why are you late?"

"There was a conference."

"You mean there was some ordinary business to be taken care of. If there had been a conference, I should have been informed along with the rest of you, even though I do not have a post in the government."

15

Duke Ting inquired whether there was one word by which the state could be made prosperous.

"Speech does not enjoy that much precision. But it is commonly said, 'Just as it is hard to be a prince, so it is not easy to be an official.' If you know the difficulties of being a prince, you are very close to rendering your country prosperous with one word."

"Is there one word which could bring my state to nought?"

"Speech does not enjoy that much precision. But it is commonly said, 'I do not like being prince, yet let no one act contrary to my word.' If it is right and no one acts contrary to it, excellent! If it is wrong and no one acts contrary to it, you will be quite close to bringing your state to nought with one word."

16

When Shen Chu-liang inquired about good government, the Master replied, "It exists when those at hand are pleased and those far away draw near."

17

When in charge of Chü-fu, Pu Shang asked about government.

"Don't seek for haste, and don't concern yourself about little advantages. If you desire haste, you will not achieve success. If you have an eye to little advantages, the big things will not get done."

18

Shen Chu-liang one day remarked to Confucius, "In my town there is one so upright that when his father stole a sheep, he, the son, testified against him."

"The upright folk in my town differ from this. The father in such a case would conceal the son, and the son would conceal the father. Uprightness lies therein."

19

Fan Hsü asked about Manhood-at-its-best.

"At home be humble; at work be respectful; with others be loyal. Even among the barbarians you may not abandon these precepts."

20

Tuan-mu Tz'u inquired, "What must a man be like to merit the title of gentleman?"

"The man who has a personal sense of shame and does not dishonor the commands of his prince when he is sent on missions to other states—such a man may be called a gentleman."

"What is next in descending order?"

"The man who is known in his clan for filial duty, and in his village for fraternal duty."

"Who comes below that?"

"The one who is unyielding in the demand that words be always truthful and deeds always fruitful—stiffly Petty Man—he, indeed, may be considered to come next."

"What would you say of those who are in government today?"

"Hm-m-m, how can we grade such halfpints?"

21

"If I can't find moderate men to deal with, I must turn to the foolhardy and the timid. The former will progress and seize upon what I have to offer; the latter will hesitate to act."

22

"The southerners have a saying which goes, 'If a man lacks constancy, he cannot be a fortuneteller or a doctor.' That's so, is it not? Now given the statement in the diviners' *Book of Changes*: 'If a man's Excellence lacks constancy, he may incur disgrace,' failure to strive for constancy simply means that one has not used the book of divination."

23

"Great Man is accommodating, but he is not one of the crowd. Petty Man is one of the crowd, but he is also a source of discord."

24

Tuan-mu Tz'u inquired, "What do you say of a man who is liked by all his townsfolk?"

"I would not find him acceptable solely for that reason."

"Suppose all his townsfolk disliked him?"

"I would not reject him solely for that reason. It is better that the competent people of the town like him, and the incompetent dislike him."

25

"Great Man is easy to serve but hard to please. If in your efforts to please him you stoop to what is contrary to System, he will not be pleased. He employs men for special tasks according to their capacities. Petty Man is hard to serve but easy to please. In your efforts to please him, he will be pleased even if you stoop to what is contrary to System. When he employs men, he expects them to be capable of anything."

26

"Great Man is dignified but not proud. Petty Man is proud but not dignified."

27

"He who is unflinching, bold, simple, natural and un-hurried approximates Manhood-at-its-best."

28

Chung Yu asked, "What must a man be like to merit the title of gentleman?"

"The man who is frank, meticulous, and accommodating may be called a gentleman. Friends are frank and meticulous; brothers are accommodating."

29

"If an able man were to instruct the people for seven years, they could indeed be used in warfare immediately thereafter."

30

"Leading an uninstructed people to war is to throw them away."

CHAPTER XIV

Yüan Hsien . . .

1

Yüan Hsien inquired about what was shameful.

"When a state is following System, one enters its pay. If one enters the pay of a state which is not following System, it is shameful."

"If a man does not insist on always being a winner, and if he is not given to boasting, petty dislikes, and inordinate desires, may he be considered to be Man-at-his-best?"

"He may be said to be engaging in difficult undertakings, but I am not sure that he is Man-at-his-best."

2

"The gentleman who prefers his own ease is no gentleman."

3

"If a state is following System, you may speak and act boldly. If it is not, let your acts be bold but your speech accommodating."

4

"The Excellent man will always have something to say, but those who do speak are not necessarily Excellent men. Man-at-his-best will be courageous, but all the courageous are not necessarily Man-at-his-best."

5

Nan-kung Kua asked Confucius, "Yi of the Hsia dynasty was a clever archer, and Ao moved a boat which was resting on dry land. Yet both of these men died before their time. On the other hand, Yü the Great and Chi both engaged personally in farming, and both rose to become rulers. Why is this?" The Master did not reply.

When his visitor had left the Master remarked, "A man like that is Great Man, for he esteems Excellence."

6

"Is it not true that there are cases where an individual is not Man-at-his-best despite the fact that he is prince? There are, however, no cases of Petty Man being Man-at-his best."

7

"Can we help requiring much of those we love? Can we help instructing those toward whom we would be loyal?"

8

"When decrees were drawn up, Pi Ch'en prepared the rough draft; Yu Chi discussed it; the Grand Receptionist Kung-sun Hui revised it; and Kung-sun Ch'iao of Tung-li gave it literary elegance."

9

Somebody asked about Kung-sun Ch'iao.

"He was gracious toward his fellow-men."

Of Tzu-hsi he said, "That fellow!"

Of Kuan Chung, the famous statesman of Ch'i, "He was like this: although he took Pien, a town of three hundred homes, from Lord Po, so that the latter was reduced to a vegetable diet, to his dying day the latter did not utter one word of resentment against Kuan Chung."

10

"To feel no resentment though poor is difficult; not to be proud though rich is easy."

11

"Meng-kung Ch'o would be excellent if he were an official of the small principalities Chao or Wei, but he may not be used as a grand gentleman in such states as T'eng or Hsüeh."

12

Chung Yu asked about the accomplished man.

"Anyone who combined the wisdom of Tsang-sun Ho, the desirelessness of Meng-kung Ch'o, the courage of Chuang-tzu of Pien, and the arts of Jan Ch'iu with an added touch from the rites and music may be considered to have been the accomplished man. But why must the accomplished man of today be like that? In the face of profit let him think of justice. In the face of danger let him offer his own life. In the face of long-standing obligations let him not forget his words of long ago. Then he may be considered the accomplished man."

13

In asking Kung-ming Chia about Kung-sun Chih the Master said, "Is it true that he neither spoke, smiled, nor took?"

"Your informant has exaggerated. When the time was right he spoke, and people did not weary of his words. When happy he smiled, and people did not weary of it. When it was proper he took things, but people did not weary of his taking."

"Like that! He couldn't have been like that!"

14

"Tsang-sun Ho, from Fang, asked that his brother Wei be recognized as sacrificer to the family's ancestors in Lu. Although it is claimed that he brought no pressure to bear against our prince, I do not believe it."

15

"Because of his lies Duke Wen of Chin must be considered less than upright. Because of his uprightness Duke Huan of Ch'i did not lie."

16

Chung Yu said, "When Duke Huan of Ch'i slew his younger brother Chiu, the latter's friend Shao Hu followed him in death, but his other friend Kuan Chung did not. Would you say it was because he had not yet achieved Manhood-at-its-best?"

"Duke Huan nine times assembled the lords of China without the use of weapons or war chariots; this was thanks to Kuan Chung. Such was Kuan Chung's superiority! He is an example of Manhood-at-its-best."

17

Tuan-mu Tz'u said, "Kuan Chung was not Manhood-at-its-best! When Duke Huan slew Chiu, he not only failed to follow his friend in death, but he also became the slayer's prime minister."

"Because Kuan Chung was his minister, Duke Huan became chief of the lords of China and brought the world to a state of rectitude, so that to this very day the people enjoy his gifts. Without Kuan Chung we should be wearing our hair down our backs and not in the topknot, and our garments would open on the left instead of on the right. He is not comparable to that miserable fellow who showed blind fidelity by strangling himself at the side of a ditch, so that he has become unknown to the world."

18

Kung-sun Chih's steward, named Chuan, accompanied him to the duke's.

"He was indeed a cultured man and deserving of his title."

19

The Master happened to mention that Duke Ling of Wei did not follow System. Thereupon Chi-sun Fei spoke up, "If he is like that, why hasn't he come to nought?"

"K'ung Yü is in charge of his guests; Prayer-leader T'o, in charge of his ancestral temple; Wang-sun Chia heads his army. Under such circumstances, why should he come to nought?"

20

"Whose language is unrestrained will have difficulty doing it all."

21

When Ch'en Heng had murdered Duke Chien, Confucius bathed both head and body and went to the court. He announced to Duke Ai, "Ch'en Heng has murdered his prince; I think he should be punished."

"Tell it to the three lords who control everything in our state."

"As the descendant of a grand gentleman I was obliged to abide by the rites and inform my prince. Now you instruct me to inform the three lords."

He did so, and they disapproved his suggestion. Confucius then repeated, "As the descendant of a grand gentleman I was obliged to abide by the rites and inform my prince."

22

Chung Yu asked how to serve a prince.
"Don't deceive him! Resist him rather."

23

"Great Man reaches complete understanding of the main issues; Petty Man reaches complete understanding of the minute details."

24

"Formerly men studied for self-improvement; today men study for the sake of appearances."

25

Ch'ü Yüan sent a messenger to Confucius, who sat down with him and inquired about his master, "Why has he sent you?"

"My master is desirous of lessening his faults, but he has not yet succeeded."

When the messenger left the Master said, "A messenger! He sends a messenger!"

26

"Do not interfere in the other man's duties."

Tseng Ts'an expressed it, "Great Man keeps his mind on his own duties."

27

"Great Man is sparing in words but prodigal in deeds."

28

"Great Man follows a three-lane path in none of which do I qualify: Manhood-at-its-best, which has no concerns; wisdom, which has no doubts; courage, which is fearless."

But Tuan-mu Tz'u spoke up, "The Master is his own path."

29

Tuan-mu Tz'u criticized some people.

"Is he then a man of the highest caliber? If he were like me he wouldn't have time for criticism."

30

"Be not concerned over men's not knowing of you; be concerned rather over your failings."

31

"Not to anticipate fraud, and not to expect falsehood, yet at the same time to be the first to perceive their presence —that is to be someone of the highest caliber!"

32

Said Wei-sheng Mu, "Why do you keep flitting from one place to another? It must be to display your eloquence!"

"I wouldn't dare do it to display eloquence. It's because I can't stand stubbornness in those I try to convince."

33

"A steed is not praised for its might, but for its thorough-bred quality."

34

Somebody asked, "What would you say of using Excellence to repay those who hate you?"

"How then will you repay Excellence? Do what is called for to repay those who hate you, and be Excellent in return for Excellence."

35

"Is it not true that no one knows of me?"

Tuan-mu Tz'u spoke up, "How is it that no one knows of you?"

"I feel no resentment toward Sky, and I do not blame men. But now that I have studied to the point of understanding everything, the one who knows of me is Sky!"

36

Kung-po Liao filed a complaint with the Chi-suns against their steward Chung Yu. Tzu-fu Ho reported this as follows: "Owing to Kung-po Liao strong suspicions have been raised against your pupil Chung Yu, but I still have enough power to see that Kung-po Liao's corpse is exposed in the public square."

"It is fate that will determine whether System prevails or fails. What is a Kung-po Liao in the face of fate?"

37

"Men of the highest caliber avoid political life completely. Those in the next lower category will move from a disordered place to one which is well governed. The next lower category will move away from sham; and the next lower category, because of something that has been said. Only seven people fall into these categories!"

38

When Chung Yu arrived to spend the night at Shih-men the gatekeeper asked, "Where are you coming from?"

"From Confucius'."

"There's a man who is undertaking something even though he knows it can't be done!"

39

One day in Wei when the Master was playing the stone gongs a man with a basket passed by the gateway and said, "He plays with great feeling!" When the playing stopped he remarked, "How petty! How stubborn! Despite the fact that nobody knows of him, he just persists in having faith in himself. We must adapt ourselves in this world! 'When the water at the ford is deep, I use the stepping-stones. When it is shallow, I lift my skirt.' "

"Naturally! He has no problems at all."

40

Chuan-sun Shih inquired, "In *The Writings of Old* it is said, 'King Kao-tsung of the Yin dynasty went into retirement and for three years did not utter a word.' What does this mean?"

"Why emphasize Kao-tsung? The men of old all did that. When their prince died, the successor went into mourning for three years, and the various officials, while tending the duties of their offices, took their orders from the prime minister for three years."

41

"If those at the top are fond of the rites, the people are easy to direct."

42

Chung Yu asked how to become Great Man.

"Stay respectful as you work at self-improvement."

"Is that all?"

"As you work at self-improvement let others feel secure."

"Is that all?"

"As you work at self-improvement bring security to all the people. But even Yao and Shun found this difficult!"

43

Yüan Jang remained crouched in Confucius' presence.
"Not to be obedient while a child; not to set a good example when grown up; and not to die when one has grown old: this is to be a source of decay!" Thereupon he struck him on the leg with his staff.

44

A lad from the village of Ch'üeh acted as the Master's messenger, and somebody asked Confucius, "Is he benefiting from such distinguished surroundings?"
"I observe him sitting in the grownups' places, and I observe him walking side by side with his elders. He's not seeking improvement. He wants to grow up quickly."

CHAPTER XV

Duke Ling of Wei . . .

1

Duke Ling of Wei asked about the alignment of an army. "I have been taught about the utensils used in the rites, but I never learned military tactics." The next day he left.

2

In Ch'en, owing to warfare, Confucius and his party were deprived of food. His followers fell so ill that they could not rise. Chung Yu then became angry and said, "Can Great Man too be reduced to the last extremity?"

"Great Man can indeed be reduced to the last extremity, but when Petty Man is so reduced he loses all self-control."

3

"Tuan-mu Tz'u, do you think of me as a man who knows about things as the result of wide study?"

"Yes. Am I wrong?"

"Yes. I have one thing, and upon it all the rest is strung." [*Compare IV, 15.*]

4

"Chung Yu, those who know about Excellence are indeed few."

5

"As for governing without interfering in minute details, Shun was the man who could do that! Why? He merely kept himself humble and his face turned due south, the recognized position of the true king."

6

Chuan-sun Shih asked what he should practice.

"Let your speech be loyal and reliable; your actions sincere and respectful. Even among the barbarians you can do this. On the other hand, if your speech is not loyal and reliable, and your actions not sincere and respectful, you will not be able to carry on either over a wide area or in a town. When you are standing, imagine that you can see these principles present as your companions. When you are in your carriage, imagine that you see them leaning against the cross-pole. In this way you will come to practice them."

Chuan-sun Shih wrote this down on his sash.

7

"Upright indeed was astrologer Yü! If the state was following System, he recorded it precisely; if not, he also recorded it precisely.

"Great Man was Ch'ü Yüan! If the state was following System, he took office; if not, he knew how to roll up his wisdom and stick it in his bosom."

8

"If we fail to speak with a man who can be spoken with, we lose a man. If we do speak with a man who cannot be spoken with, our words go for nought. The wise lose neither man nor words."

9

"The strong-willed gentleman who is Manhood-at-its-best never seeks life at the expense of Manhood-at-its-best, but there are cases where his life is given for the accomplishment of Manhood-at-its-best."

10

Tuan-mu Tz'u inquired how to become Manhood-at-its-best.

"When the workman wishes to do a good job, he must first sharpen his tools. So, in your case, no matter what state you inhabit, serve only the grand gentlemen of highest standing, make friends only with those gentlemen who are Manhood-at-its-best."

11

Yüan Hui inquired how to govern a state.

"Use the Hsia calendar. Ride in a Yin carriage. Wear a Chou hat. When there is music, let it be that of Shun. Banish the songs of Cheng, and keep away from the eloquent, for the songs of Cheng are depraved and the eloquent are dangerous."

12

"If a man does not give thought to problems which are still distant, he will be worried by them when they come nearer."

13

"The end has indeed arrived! I have yet to meet a man as fond of Excellence as he is of outward appearances."

14

"Did Tsang-sun Ch'en play the sneak in the position which he held? I should say that he did, for despite the fact that he knew that Chan Huo was a man of the highest caliber, he did not have him as a colleague."

15

"If a man is sparing in his reproaches of others while he heaps them upon himself, he will certainly keep away resentments."

16

"I can do absolutely nothing for the man who will not bring me his problems."

17

"Those who can be in a group all day and, without speaking of justice, give themselves over solely to their own little kindnesses—such people would certainly have difficulty achieving the ideal I set."

18

"He whose very substance is justice, whose actions are governed by the rites, whose participation in affairs is compliant, and whose crowning perfection is reliability—that man is Great Man."

19

"Great Man complains about his own inabilities, not about people's ignorance of himself."

20

"Great Man's concern is that he may die without a good name."

21

"Great Man demands it of himself; Petty Man, of others."

22

"Great Man, out of a sense of pride, does not engage in strife; out of consideration for the group as a whole he does not join cliques."

23

"Great Man does not accept a man for his words alone; he does not reject a suggestion because of the man alone."

24

Tuan-mu Tz'u inquired, "Is there one word that will keep us on the path to the end of our days?"
"Yes. Reciprocity! What you do not wish yourself, do not unto others."

25

"I approach others with neither blame nor praise in my heart. If I do praise anybody, it is after having tried him. Through such an attitude toward their people, the three dynasties have traveled the straight path."

26

"In my time I have come upon an astrologer who, when in doubt, would record nothing, and a horse owner who would get others to break in his stock. But such people no longer exist today, do they?"

27

"Just as a clever remark can ruin another's Excellence, so, if there is the slightest impatience, a grand scheme can be ruined."

28

"If everyone dislikes it, it must be looked into. If everyone likes it, it must be looked into."

29

"Man can make System great; it isn't System which makes man great."

30

"Not to alter one's faults is to be faulty indeed."

31

"I once went all day without food and all night without sleep to enable me to think. I found no advantage in it; it's best to study."

32

"Great Man calculates in terms of System, not in terms of the earning of a living! Agriculture is inspired by the fear of hunger; study, by an interest in salary. Great Man is concerned about System, not about poverty!"

33

"A man's knowledge may be sufficient for a post but his superiority insufficient for maintaining it, so although he gets the post he is sure to lose it. Both knowledge and superiority may be sufficient, but if he administers it without dignity the people will not be respectful. Both knowledge and superiority may be sufficient, and he may administer it with dignity, but if he acts contrary to the rites, he is not yet competent."

34

"Great Man gives his approval not to techniques but to the capacity for great responsibility. Petty Man does just the opposite."

35

"Manhood-at-its-best is of greater importance to the people than either fire or water. I have seen fire and water cause deaths, but I have never seen Manhood-at-its-best cause them."

36

"He who is Manhood-at-its-best does not need to make way for the teacher!"

37

"Great Man does not show a blind persistence in his practice of uprightness."

38

"As you serve your prince give precedence to his interest; think of your reward last."

39

"Instruction recognizes no castes."

40

"Those who follow different roads cannot take counsel with one another."

41

"It is enough that one's words express fully one's thought."

42

When the maestro Mien, who was blind, arrived on a visit, upon his reaching the steps the Master said, "Here are the steps." When he reached the mat, "Here's the mat." When they had seated themselves, "So-and-so is here, and so-and-so is here."

When the guest had gone, Chuan-sun Shih inquired, "Is that the proper way to talk with maestros, all of whom are blind?"

"Yes. This is the proper way to lead maestros."

CHAPTER XVI

The Chis . . .

1

When the Chis of Lu were about to attack the state of Chuan-yü, Jan Ch'iu and Chung Yu sought an interview with Confucius and reported, "The Chis are about to have an incident with Chuan-yü."

"Jan Ch'iu, this is your fault! Of old, our former kings looked upon the Chuan-yü as the chiefs of Tung-meng, and they were situated within the confines of our state of Lu. They are, then, natives of our state. Why are they to be attacked?"

"Our prince desires it. Neither of us wants it."

"Jan Ch'iu, the astrologer Chou Jen used to say, 'Let the strong ones in the host enter the line. Let the incompetent desist!' Of what use are counselors who do not uphold and support a state when it is endangered or when it is tottering? Further, your reasoning is erroneous. Whose fault is it when the tiger or the wild bull escapes its pen, or when the tortoise or the valued gem is damaged in its box?"

"Yes, but today those Chuan-yü are strong and close to Pi, an important city of the Chis. If they are not attacked today, later on they will certainly be a source of concern for our descendants."

"Isn't it true, Jan Ch'iu, that Great Man dislikes to yield and say, 'It must be done because it is desired'? For my part, I have been taught that the head of a state or the head of a family is not concerned about numbers; he is concerned about misapportionments. He is not concerned about poverty, but about insecurity. Perhaps I may put it this way: Where there is apportionment there is no poverty. When there is harmony the number is sufficient. Where security reigns there are no troubles. But when, under the circumstances you describe, men at a distance do not submit, we attract them through our refinement and Excellence. Once they have been attracted, we give them security. Today you, Chung Yu and Jan Ch'iu, are the prince's ministers. Distant people, not being submissive, cannot be attracted. Our country is tumbling and splitting up to the point that it is impossible to preserve it. Yet movements of troops within our state have been advised. I fear that the concerns of the Chis are not with the Chuan-yü but with their own council."

2

"When the world is following System, then the rites, the music, punitive expeditions, and attacks are all determined by the Son of Sky, that is, the king. Otherwise, these things emanate from the feudal lords. When they emanate from the feudal lords they will probably last ten generations. If it's from the grand gentlemen, they will last five generations. A family steward can control the destinies of a realm for three generations. But if the world is following System, affairs will not be in the hands of the grand gentlemen, and ordinary men will not be criticizing the state."

3

"Officials in Lu have not been employed by the legitimate ducal line of the state for five generations; affairs have been in the hands of the grand gentlemen for four generations. Hence these descendants of Duke Huan of Ch'i are weakening."

4

"Three friends benefit us; three harm us. The upright friend, the devoted, and the learned benefit us. The fawning friend, the flattering, and the too eloquent harm us."

5

"Three pleasures benefit us; three harm us. The pleasure of keeping to the proprieties of the rites and music, of speaking of others' competencies, of having many friends of the highest caliber benefit us. The pleasure of reveling in pleasures, in idle wandering, in the delights of the banquet table harm us."

6

"When attending a prince, you are subject to three errors: speaking before spoken to, which is called impetuousness; not to reply when spoken to, which is called reticence; speaking without observing his facial expression, which is called blindness."

7

"Great Man avoids three things: sexual intercourse while still too young and before his pulse has settled down; fighting, once he has grown up and his pulse has become strong; further acquisition, once he has grown old and his pulse has weakened."

8

"There are three things of which Great Man stands in awe: the commands of Sky, important people, the words of the sages. Petty Man, not knowing the commands of Sky, does not stand in awe of them; he is disrespectful to important people; he mocks the words of the sages."

9

"Those born with an understanding of the universe belong to the highest type of humanity. Those who understand it as the result of study come second. Those who study it with great difficulty come third. And the people, who find it too difficult to attempt study, come last."

10

"There are nine things of which Great Man must be mindful: to see when he looks, to hear when he listens, to have a facial expression of gentleness, to have an attitude of humility, to be loyal in speech, to be respectful in service, to inquire when in doubt, to think of the difficulties when angry, to think of justice when he sees an advantage."

11

"I have seen and heard of men who, upon finding competence, strove with might and main to equal it; others who, catching sight of incompetence, withdrew as if removing a hand from boiling water. I have heard of men living in retirement from active life in order to seek what they desired most. I have heard of them doing what was right in order to achieve their way of life. I have yet, however, to meet such men."

12

Duke Ching of Ch'i possessed one thousand teams of horses, but on the day he died the people could find no Excellence of his to praise. Po-i and Shu-ch'i died of hunger at the foot of Mt. Shou-yang, and the people praise them to the present day. Is the following line from *The Poems* a reference to such a situation: "Truly not for wealth, only indeed for difference in quality"?

13

Ch'en K'ang inquired of Confucius' son Li, "Has your father taught you any differently than he did us?"

"Not yet. But one day when he was standing alone and I was passing quickly through the courtyard, he said, 'Have you studied *The Poems?*' 'Not yet,' I replied. 'Well,' said he, 'if you don't study *The Poems* you won't be able to carry on a conversation.' So I withdrew and studied *The Poems*. Another day the same situation was repeated and he asked. 'Have you studied the rites?' And I replied, 'Not yet.' He continued, 'If you don't study the rites, you will not be able to play your proper rôle.' So I withdrew and studied the rites. I have been taught these two things."

Ch'en K'ang withdrew and was quite happy as he said, "From one question I have discovered three things. I have learned about *The Poems;* I have learned about the rites; I have learned of the distance which Great Man keeps between himself and his son."

14

The wife of a prince is called Lady by her husband. She calls herself Child. The people call her the Prince's Lady. When she is mentioned to officials of another state she is called Our Princess. When people of another state mention her, they too say the Prince's Lady.

CHAPTER XVII

Yang Hu . . .

1

Yang Hu wanted to receive Confucius, and when he did not go to visit, he sent him a suckling pig. Confucius then went to call upon him, after choosing a moment when he would not be at home, but he met him along the way. Yang Hu then said, "Come! Let us have a talk. Can we call a person Manhood-at-its-best if he lets his state wallow in confusion while he keeps a jewel of wisdom concealed within his bosom?"

"No."

"Can we call a man wise if he is prompt to miss every opportunity when he really likes to do things?"

"No."

"The days and months are indeed passing, and the years play no favorites!"

"You're right. I'll accept public office."

2

"In our natures we approximate one another; habits put us further and further apart.

"The only ones who do not change are sages and idiots."

3

On arriving at Wu-ch'eng the Master heard a song accompanied by a cither, and he smiled, saying, "Why are they using an axe to kill that chicken when a hatchet would be better?"

Yen Yen then spoke up, "A long time ago I heard the Master say this: 'As a result of his study of System, Great Man comes to love his fellow men; Petty Man from such study becomes disdainful.' "

"My pupils, Yen Yen is right. That remark of mine was made only in jest."

4

When Kung-shan Fu-pan revolted at Pi, he summoned the Master, and he wanted to go.

Chung Yu, however, was displeased and said, "You've never gone to anyone else! Why must you go to Kung-shan?"

"He certainly isn't summoning me to no purpose! If he would put me to work, I should rear a Chou dynasty here in the East!"

5

Chuan-sun Shih asked about Manhood-at-its-best.

"He who in this world can practice five things may indeed be considered Man-at-his-best."

"What are they?"

"Humility, magnanimity, sincerity, diligence, and graciousness. If you are humble, you will not be laughed at. If you are magnanimous, you will attract many to your side. If you are sincere, people will trust you. If you are diligent, you will be successful. If you are gracious, you will get along well with your subordinates."

6

When Pi Hsi of the Chin state summoned him, the Master wanted to go.

Chung Yu then said, "Long ago I heard the Master say this: 'Great Man does not enter the home of the man who is personally bad.' Now, since Pi Hsi is in revolt at Chung-mou, how can you go there?"

"You're right, I said that. But isn't it also said, 'What is really hard cannot be made thin by rubbing; what is really white does not become black by dyeing'? Am I to be hung up and left uneaten like some gourds?"

7

"Chung Yu, have you learned the six terms for the six defects?"

"Not yet."

"Stay, and I'll tell you. To be fond of Manhood-at-its-best but not of learning: stupidity. To be fond of wisdom but not of learning: sloth. To be fond of reliability but not of learning: decadence. To be fond of uprightness but not of learning: rudeness. To be fond of acts of courage but not of learning: rebelliousness. To be fond of steadfastness but not of learning: foolhardiness."

8

"My pupils, why do none of you study these poems? Through *The Poems* minds can be aroused, a point of vantage gained, sociability exercised, resentments expressed, one's father and one's prince served, and one's knowledge increased in respect to the names of birds, animals, plants, and trees." And turning to his son Li he continued, "Have you learned the first two sections of *The Poems?* Any man who hasn't faces a brick wall!"

9

"By rites we certainly don't mean gems and silks! And by music we certainly don't mean bells and drums! These are merely the externals."

10

"Those who are outwardly strict but inwardly lax may be compared with Petty Man. They may be compared with the burglar who climbs or pierces our walls!"

11

"Continuous readaptation to suit the whims of others undermines Excellence."

12

"To engage in gossip is to cast aside Excellence."

13

"It's impossible to serve the prince with an inferior colleague! Before getting the post he will be fearful of getting it, and once he gets it he will be fearful of losing it. Being foolishly fearful of losing it, there are no ends to which he will not go."

14

"The people of old had three defects which are probably lacking today. The foolhardy among the ancients were venturesome; in the present they are slothful. The proud among the ancients were straightforward; in the present they are quarrelsome. The stupid among the ancients were upright; those of the present are merely cheaters."

15

"Clever talk and a domineering manner have little to do with being Man-at-his-best."

16

"I dislike the way the clever talker upsets states and homes, just as I dislike purple's encroachment upon red and the way the tunes of Cheng have played riot with elegant music."

17

"I prefer to say nothing."

Then Tuan-mu Tz'u spoke up. "If the Master says nothing, how shall we transmit him?"

"Sky says nothing! Yet the four seasons proceed under its sway, and all creation comes into being thanks to it. Sky says nothing!"

18

When Ju Pei sought an interview Confucius excused himself on the grounds of illness. As his messenger was leaving the house Confucius took up his cither and strummed a song so that he could hear.

19

Tsai Yü inquired whether the three years' period of mourning was not too long. If Great Man fails to follow the rites for three years, they would certainly fall to ruin. If he has no music for three years, it too would certainly crumble. Let the period of mourning be terminated once the grain cribs have been emptied and filled and the rounds made of the various woods used to make fire, i.e., one year.

The Master answered him, "Would you feel secure, after only one year, to eat that rice of yours and wear those silks?"

"Yes."

"Well, if you feel secure, do so. But when Great Man is in mourning, he does not find good food to his liking; he is not happy on hearing music; he is not satisfied with his normal resting place. Hence he does none of these things. Today, however, if you feel secure, go and do them."

When he had gone the Master said, "Tsai Yü is not Manhood-at-its-best. Since it is only after three years that a child quits the bosom of its parents, the three years' period of mourning is general throughout the world. Was Tsai Yü loved by his parents for three years?"

20

"To eat one's fill all day long without directing the mind to anything is, indeed, to be in difficulties! Even those who spend all their time at intricate games are to be reckoned of higher caliber."

21

Chung Yu inquired, "Does Great Man esteem courage?"

"Great Man is given to justice and assigns to it first place. If Great Man possessed courage but not justice, there would be rebellions. In the case of Petty Man, there would be pilferings."

22

Tuan-mu Tz'u inquired, "Are there really persons whom Great Man dislikes?"

"Yes. He dislikes those who divulge the faults of others. He dislikes those who, being of low condition, malign their superiors. He dislikes the courageous who do not follow the rites. He dislikes those of little intelligence who react without thinking. But you, Tuan-mu Tz'u, do you too have some persons you dislike?"

"I dislike those who think transcription is knowledge, who think noncompliance is courage, who think tale-bearing is uprightness."

23

"Only women and Petty Man are hard to have around the house. If you become close to them, they turn noncompliant. If you keep them at a distance, they turn resentful."

24

"It is all over for the man of forty who is held in aversion."

CHAPTER XVIII

The Viscount of Wei . . .

1

Under the Yin dynasty the Viscount of Wei left the capital, the Viscount of Chi was enslaved, and Pi-kan was put to death because he remonstrated with the king. This is why Confucius said one day, "Under the Yin there were three examples of Manhood-at-its-best."

2

Chan Huo was three times deposed from his position in charge of the prison, and someone said to him, "Can't you make up your mind to leave the state?"

"If I am to serve men uprightly, where could I go and not be deposed three times? If I am to serve men dishonestly, why must I leave my native state?"

3

As he was awaiting Confucius, Duke Ching of Ch'i remarked, "I can't receive him with the same protocol as that used for a member of the Chi family of Lu. I will treat him as ranking between the Chi and Meng families."

Later, the duke's remark was, "I am too old to undertake the reforms. I can't use him." Confucius then left.

4

When those in Ch'i sent the dancing girls to Lu, Chi-sun Ssu accepted them, and for three days no court was held. Confucius then left.

5

Lu T'ung, the madman of Ch'u, sang as he passed by Confucius, "O phoenix, how Excellence has declined! Yet it's not right to remonstrate about what has passed; the future is still to be overtaken. But things are as they are, and those who operate the government today are dangerous."

Confucius got out of his carriage and wished to speak with him. But the man fled quickly, so that Confucius did not succeed in talking to him.

6

While Ch'ang-chü and Chieh-ni were tilling together Confucius rode by and had Chung Yu ask them where the fording place was.

Ch'ang-chü inquired, "Who is that holding the reins?"

"It's Confucius."

"Do you mean Confucius of Lu?"

"Yes."

"He knows the fording place."

He then inquired of Chieh-ni, who replied, "Who are you?"

"I'm Chung Yu."

"Are you a pupil of Confucius of Lu?"

"Yes."

"Flowing on and on, the whole world is like you. And who is going to change it? Instead of following in the train of a gentleman who flees from men wouldn't you do better to join with those who flee the world completely and live as hermits?" And he went on hoeing.

Chung Yu then left and reported. Confucius replied sadly, "We can't be one with the birds and beasts. And if I don't join with the wanderers, with whom shall I join? If the world were following System, I should not be doing my part to reform it."

7

As Chung Yu was traveling with Confucius, he fell behind and met with an old man who was carrying a basket over his shoulder by means of a staff. He inquired of the old man, "Have you seen the Master?"

"You're a man who does no physical work and you can't tell one kind of grain from another. Who is your master?" Then setting down his staff, he pulled some weeds, and Chung Yu stood politely with his hands joined.

He kept Chung Yu with him for the night, killed a chicken and prepared some millet for food, and introduced to him his two sons. The following day, Chung Yu departed and reported the matter. The Master said, "He was a hermit." And he bade Chung Yu return for a visit with him. But when Chung Yu arrived, the hermit had disappeared.

Thereupon Chung Yu spoke as follows: "To fail to serve in the government is not right. Just as the restraints of maturity and youth must be preserved, so must also the right relation between prince and subject be maintained. Desire to maintain one's own personal integrity can lead to the disruption of a greater principle. Great Man takes office in the government; he does what is right. But it has long been known that System is not being followed."

8

The following lived as private citizens: Po-i, Shu-ch'i, Yü Chung, I-i, Chu Chang, Chan Huo, and Shao-lien. The Master said of them, "Po-i and Shu-ch'i did not flinch in their resolution; they have never disgraced themselves."

Of Chan Huo and Shao-lien he said that they had lacked resolution and incurred self-disgrace, but it was simply that they were men who spoke in accord with high principles and acted in keeping with their concerns. He said of Yü Chung and I-i that they lived privately and remained silent; they maintained a personal purity and their abstention from public office was in keeping with prevailing conditions. And he continued, "I am different from these men. I take life as it comes."

9

The Grand Musician of Lu, Chih, left and went to Ch'i; the one who played at the second meal of the day, Kan, went to Ch'u; the one who played at the third, Liao, went to Ts'ai; the fourth, Ch'üeh, went to Ch'in. The drum-beater, Fang-shu, went north of the river; the twirler of the hand drum, Wu, went down into the valley of the Han River;

the Assistant Musician, Yang, and Hsiang, who played the stones, went out to sea.

10

The Duke of Chou once said to the Duke of Lu, "The prince does not neglect the members of his family; he does not let the chief ministers become resentful because they are not consulted. He does not reject his old friends except for serious reasons. He does not expect one individual to be capable of all things."

11

Under the Chou there were eight gentlemen, four sets of twins by one mother: Po-ta, Po-kuo, Chung-tu, Chung-hu, Shu-yeh, Shu-hsia, Chi-sui, and Chi-kua.

CHAPTER XIX

Chuan-sun Shih . . .

1

Chuan-sun Shih said, "I certainly give full approval to the gentleman who in the face of peril offers his life; who, when about to acquire something, thinks of right; who keeps respect in mind as he sacrifices, and grief in mind as he mourns."

2

Chuan-sun Shih said, "How are we to evaluate the man who, while maintaining Excellence, does not further its influence; or the man who, having put his faith in System, is not sincere?"

3

Pu Shang's pupils asked Chuan-sun Shih about the formation of friendships, so he asked them, "What does Pu Shang say on the subject?"

"He says, 'Make friendships with those you approve, and reject those whom you disapprove.' "

"That differs from what I was taught. Great Man, although giving his respect to men of the highest caliber, maintains a proper regard for all. While reserving his praises for the competent, he is compassionate toward the less able. If I am a man of the highest caliber, there is no one toward whom I am unable to maintain a proper regard. If I am not a man of the highest caliber, my fellow-men will reject me. There must be no rejection of my fellow-men."

4

Pu Shang said, "Even the lesser doctrines contain something instructive for us, but over the years I fear that they will leave us wanting. Hence Great Man does not practice them."

5

Pu Shang said, "He who is daily conscious of his lacks and every month checks to see that he is neglecting none of his abilities—that man is indeed fond of learning."

6

Pu Shang said, "Remain sincere in purpose while studying widely, continue to think while posing frank and open questions. Therein lies Manhood-at-its-best."

7

Pu Shang said, "Just as artisans inhabit the market place to ply their trades, so Great Man studies to improve his doctrine."

8

Pu Shang said, "Petty Man always glosses over his own faults."

9

Pu Shang said, "There are three facets to Great Man. Looked at from a distance he seems stern; at close range he is pleasant; as we listen to his words they are clear-cut."

10

Pu Shang said, "Great Man does not work a people until he has won their confidence, otherwise they will feel that he is severe with them. He does not remonstrate with a superior until he has won his confidence, otherwise he will feel that he is maligned."

11

Pu Shang said, "Who keeps strictly within bounds when Excellence is of great importance may waver in cases where it is of lesser importance."

12

Yen Yen said, "Pu Shang's pupils know how to sprinkle and sweep, how to answer questions, and how to enter and withdraw. But these are mere details; they are totally lacking in the fundamentals. What can we do with them?"

When this was reported to Pu Shang, he replied, "Yen Yen is mistaken! The ways of Great Man are transmitted to the superior, but from the inferior they are withheld. People are of different types, as are plants and trees. In the ways of Great Man there must be no deceit. Only the sage possesses them in all completeness!"

13

Pu Shang said, "If there is spare time while holding office, let it be given to study. If there is spare time while studying, let it be given to holding office."

14

Chung Yu said, "Let mourning stop after full expression of our grief."

15

Chung Yu said, "Chuan-sun Shih is a friend of mine. He is capable of many difficult things, but he is not yet Manhood-at-its-best."

16

Tseng Ts'an said, "Chuan-sun Shih makes a fine impression, but it is hard to achieve Manhood-at-its-best at his side."

17

Tseng Ts'an said, "I once heard it said by the Master that even if a man had never once done a thing wholeheartedly, he must do so at the death of a parent."

18

Tseng Ts'an said, "In regard to Chung-sun Su's observance of filial duty I once heard the Master say that with one exception it would be possible for others to equal him. However, he made no changes either in his father's advisers or in his policies. This would be hard for another to equal."

19

When the Mengs put Yang Fu in charge of the prison, he asked Tseng Ts'an how he should administer the post.

"Since our rulers have lost contact with System, the people have gone astray for some time. If you succeed in feeling things as they do, you will have compassion for those in your prison. You shall take no joy in their punishment."

20

Tuan-mu Tz'u said, "King Chou of the Yin dynasty was not as black as he has been painted, so Great Man shuns low company for fear that all the evils of the world will be imputed to him."

21

Tuan-mu Tz'u said, "The faults of Great Man may be compared to eclipses of the sun and moon. While they are being committed everyone sees them, but once he changes everyone gazes up at him in respect."

22

Kung-sun Ch'ao of Wei asked Tuan-mu Tz'u, "Under whom did Confucius study?"

"Before the ways of Kings Wen and Wu of our Chou dynasty had degenerated, those of the highest caliber knew the important principles and those of a lower caliber knew the lesser matters. No one failed to know some aspect of the ways of Kings Wen and Wu. So, the Master did his studying of anyone and everyone. He did not have a formal teacher."

23

Shu-sun Chou-ch'ou said to the grand gentlemen at court, "Tuan-mu Tz'u is of higher caliber than Confucius."

When Tzu-fu Ho reported this to Tuan-mu Tz'u, he replied, "Let me use for comparison a dwelling with its surrounding wall. The wall around my house is shoulder high, so that anyone can look over and see its good points. The Master's is considerably higher. Unless one enters by the gate, it is impossible to see the beauties of the ancestral temple, the richness of the appointments. And at times there are indeed few who reach the gate! The gentleman's remarks are uncalled for!"

24

When Shu-sun Chou-ch'ou spoke ill of Confucius, Tuan-mu Tz'u replied, "There are no grounds. One may not speak ill of Confucius. The excellences of others may be compared to the hills and mounds over which it is still possible to pass. Confucius, however, is both the sun and the moon; and over these we cannot pass. Even though a man should cut himself off from them, what harm would he be doing to the sun and the moon? He would merely display far and wide his own ignorance of proportions."

25

Ch'en K'ang said to Tuan-mu Tz'u, "You are too humble. Confucius wasn't of higher caliber than you!"

"Just as Great Man may be considered wise because of some one word, so, because of some one word, one may be considered ignorant. Our inability to reach the peak occupied by the Master may be compared to our inability to reach the sky by stairs. If the Master had been in charge of a state or a household, the situation would have been such that what he would establish was established. When he would lead into System, there was instant progress in that direction; when he wished to bring tranquility, it arrived immediately; when he organized a movement, all acted in one accord. His life was a source of splendor; his death, of grief. So how can we hope to reach the eminence he occupies?"

CHAPTER XX

Yao spoke . . .

1

The Sage-King Yao spoke thus: "This do I declare to you, Shun. Sky has set its finger upon you; long may it remain. To the end of the world may Sky's rewards to you be everlasting."

On the same note Shun commanded Yü.

It has also been said, "Child that I am, I, T'ang of the Yin dynasty, make bold to sacrifice a black bull. I make bold to declare to the august departed emperors: 'The guilty I dare not pardon. As the emperors' servant I do not act in secret; the decree resides in the hearts of the emperors. If I personally prove guilty, it is not to be imputed to all. Rather, if the others have guilt, the blame is to be imputed to me.' "

Also, "Let the Chou dynasty flourish, and may the competent be enriched thereby. Though there may be Chou relatives, it is best to use an individual who is Man-at-his-best. Then if the people come to have faults, the blame can be imputed to their ruler. Give careful attention to weights and measures, examine the laws and regulations, restore offices which have been abolished. Thereby the administration of the world will be set in motion. Restore states which have been destroyed, see that broken family lines are re-established, raise to position men who have been neglected. Thereby the people of the world will turn to you. Hold of high importance the people, stocks of food, mourning for the departed, as also the sacrifices to them. If you are indulgent, you will win the mass. If you are reliable, the people will put their confidence in you. If you are diligent, you will be successful. If you consider only the public interest, there will be contentment."

2

Chuan-sun Shih inquired, "What must be done to prepare oneself for service in the government?"

"Esteem the five high qualities, and avoid the four evils, then you can serve in the government."

"What are the five high qualities?"

"Great Man is gracious without bribery. He can work people without making them resentful. He has desires, but he is not greedy. He is dignified, but not proud. He inspires awe, but he is not brutal."

"What do you mean by the first of these?"

"To treat as advantageous what the people find advantageous, isn't this being gracious without bribery? If we put to work only those who can properly be put to work, who will be resentful? If a man, out of desire for Manhood-at-its-best, achieves it, how can he be greedy? Great Man, without regard to quantity and size, is not slothful—isn't that to be dignified but not proud? Great Man keeps his clothes and hat straight and his glances respectful. And because of his seriousness, people feel a reverence as they look up at him—isn't this to inspire awe without brutality?"

"What are the four evils?"

"To put to death for the lack of instructions: this is cruelty. To expect accomplishment without proper advisement: this is outrageousness. To insist upon completion after instructions to proceed slowly: this is deterioration. To promise a reward but to begrudge its payment: this is pettiness."

3

"Who fails to recognize fate can never become Great Man. Who fails to follow the rites can never play his proper rôle. Who does not know the value of words will never come to understand his fellow-men."

Chinese Dynastic Successions

Hsia—prehistoric North China.
Shang (or Yin) ends around 1100 B.C.
Chou:
    The Annals (*Ch'un-ch'iu*) 722–481 B.C.
    Warring States, 403–250 B.C.
Ch'in (or Ts'in) 221–207 B.C.—founding of the empire.
First Han, 202 B.C.—A.D. 8. Buddhism arrives.
    Wang Mang, A.D. 9–23.
Second Han, A.D. 23–220.
Three Kingdoms:
    Wei, 220–265—North China.
    Shu, 221–263—West China.
    Wu, 222–280—South China.
Chin (or Tsin), 265–316—all China.
    317–420—South China (sixteen kingdoms, contemporaneous or successive, in the North).
Southern and northern dynasties:
    Five successive dynasties in South, 420–589.
    Northern Wei (Turks) and its four successors in North, 399–581.
Sui, 581–618—China reunited.
T'ang, 618–907.
Five dynasties and ten kingdoms (contemporaneous or successive), 907–979.
Sung, 960–1126—all China.
    1127–1279—South China.
        Liao (Kitan), 916–1125—Manchuria.
        Hsi Hsia (Tangut), 1032–1227—Kansu.
        Chin or Kin (Juchen), 1115–1234—North China.
Yüan (Mongols), 1279–1368—all China.
Ming, 1368–1644.
Ch'ing (or Ts'ing) (Manchus), 1644–1912.
Chinese Republic 1912–
    Chiang goes to Formosa 1949–

Bibliography

Readers interested in deepening their acquaintance with China's classical tradition are referred to the following books:

H. G. CREEL: *Confucius* (1949).
JAMES LEGGE: *The Chinese Classics,* 8 vols. (1865-1895).
    Li Ki, 2 vols. (1885).
    The Sacred Books of China (1879), contains translation of *Filial Duty Classic.*
    The Yi King (1882).
JOHN STEELE: *The I-li,* 2 vols. (1917).
ARTHUR WALEY: *The Analects of Confucius* (1938).
    The Book of Songs (1937).

Index of Subjects

This book, like most others that have come to us out of antiquity, is informal in presentation. The contents are incomplete and the subjects undeveloped because they were inspired by very specific occasions whose contexts form part of the varying oral school tradition in the Far East. The original form has been retained here in order that the reader may have the pleasure of digging out for himself the guides to wise action which this rich book contains. The following is an incomplete list of interesting subjects treated: